Thanks for the Memory

Thanks for the Memory

British Railways working steam

Mike Esau

· RAILWAY HERITAGE ·
from
The NOSTALGIA Collection

First published in 2005

British Library Cataloguing in Publication Data

A catalogue record for this book is available from the British Library.

ISBN 1 85794 245 0

Silver Link Publishing Ltd
The Trundle
Ringstead Road
Great Addington
Kettering
Northants NN14 4BW

Tel/Fax: 01536 330588
email: sales@nostalgiacollection.com
Website: www.nostalgiacollection.com

Printed and bound in Great Britain

Half title **Euston: 'Princess Coronation' 4-6-2 No 46225 *Duchess of Gloucester***
Watched by a lone enthusiast, the 'Duchess' slips momentarily as it begins the climb out of the station with a midday train for Scotland.

Page 2 **Near Burton & Holme: two Stanier '8F' 2-8-0s, No 48010 leading**
On a gloomy winter day the two locomotives are producing a spectacular exhaust as they struggle northward up the gradient near Burton & Holme with a heavy permanent way train of track panels.

Title page **Newcastle Emlyn: '5700' 0-6-0PT No 9787, 1960**
Where my love of railways began – during the war, in order to escape the bombing in London, my mother and I moved down to live with Welsh relations in Newcastle Emlyn. In an effort to keep me amused my mother used to take me to the station to see the trains. I still remember sitting on this platform waiting for the branch train to come in from Pencader, then being lifted up on to the footplate of the Pannier tank. The smell of hot oil and steam is unforgettable! Passenger services ceased in 1952 but the line continued to be busy for freight traffic, mostly coal, cattle feed and petroleum spirit for the local Esso depot. No 9787 has just arrived with the daily working from Carmarthen.

Above left **Near Attymon Junction, Loughrea branch, Eire: 'J15' 0-6-0 No 583, September 1962**
As you can readily see by the unfamiliar locomotive and the lightly laid 5ft 3in-gauge track, which is being attended to by the permanent way men, this picture, taken by my wife Alison, is not on British Railways but CIE. However, it does show me at work with my camera. Judging by the steam leak on the 'J15', I think I would have obtained a much better result if I had stayed on Alison's side of the line!

Contents

Opposite below **Wadebridge: '0298' 2-4-0WT No 30586, September 1961**
Alison has been invited on to the footplate of the station pilot, Beattie 'Well tank' No 30586 – she is clearly enjoying the experience! Unfortunately No 30586 was the only one of the three 'Well tanks' still working at that time not to be preserved.

Right **Petworth: 'Q' 0-6-0 No 30544, 5 November 1960**
Among the best memories of the working steam era was travel on the brake-van of a pick-up goods train along a country branch line. On this beautiful autumn day, my brother David (on the right), lifelong friend Gerald ('Gerry') Siviour (left) and I have been issued with a permit to travel from Midhurst to Pulborough. No 30544, which looks as if it has recently been through Eastleigh works, is shunting some wagons in the station yard before continuing its journey.

Introduction

When Bob Hope died not so long ago, his theme song was broadcast in the many tributes paid to him at the time. So it was that *Thanks for the Memory* seemed to be the perfect title for this book, which recalls, through the photographs, memories of the working steam era on British Railways. As the words of the song so aptly say:

'...Oh, well, it was swell while it lasted; we did have fun and no harm done. And thanks for the memory...'*

Yes it was great fun photographing the steam era, whatever the weather. But with so much to see, so many places to go, there was not enough time or money to achieve every objective. Certainly it was a harmless activity, although of course many could not resist the temptation to 'bunk' sheds without a permit, such was their draw. But in general, enthusiasts of the day were well-behaved and respectful of authority. In turn the railway administration was very tolerant of us, for example issuing permits for brake-van travel on lines closed to passenger traffic or arranging complicated railtours behind unusual locomotives. So far as I was concerned, the most valued facility was the issue of a lineside pass for photography, which was a tremendous help in the quest for the best pictures.

Before the era of the international terrorist and the problems now associated with drink and drugs, enthusiasts were able to derive pleasure from their pastime without hindrance or question, spending hours observing or photographing trains at stations or along the line. When I was up in London last year, it came home to me how the world had changed when I saw at St Pancras station a notice from the train operating company headed 'Our Policy on Aggression'.

But this book is about more relaxed times on the railway, so I have grouped the photographs into areas that I feel encapsulate memories of steam. Thus there are pictures of locomotive sheds, steam in various parts of the country, in the seasons of the year, and so on. Before I was married I lived in New Malden, close to the main line from Waterloo, so naturally most of my early memories are of the 'Southern', although, as I have related in the caption to the picture on page 4, my lifelong passion for railways began on the Great Western Railway in west Wales.

As a young, budding railway photographer, with a limited income, the cost of film was a major consideration. However, because I have always used medium-format cameras with fewer exposures per roll of film, there was the discipline of trying to make every shot count. On the subject of cameras, most of the pictures in this book were taken with a Zeiss Super Ikonta I bought in West Germany in 1956, a couple of Voightlander Bessa IIs, supplemented by another Super Ikonta and a Bronica S 6cm x 6cm SLR. Later in the book I relate how one of the Bessa IIs let me down at the beginning of a holiday to Scotland – every railway photographer's nightmare.

To get to faraway places like Scotland or to the best locations quite close to home, some form of personal transport was a necessity, so like others of my generation I started by cycling to various places, usually on the Southern Region. A regular day trip from my home when I was in my early teens was down the A3 road to Guildford, then to Horsham via Cranleigh, along to Three Bridges, up to Redhill, and thence back via the hilly A217, a distance of about 70 miles. Although it has now been superseded by a modern Marin machine with 21 gears, I still have my old bike with its three-speed Sturmey Archer hub gear and wonder how on earth I managed to ride so far on it in all weathers! Later on I bought my first Lambretta scooter, an LI 125 Series II, which I kept for a couple of years before exchanging it for the more powerful TV 175 Series II, depicted on page 36. Once my son Richard arrived in 1964, a car was a necessity, so after that trips were made in comfort in an Austin 1100.

Even with the freedom of personal transport, how did you choose where to go? The West Country was an obvious choice, though not so easy to reach as now, with the advent of motorways. A journey down to Cornwall really was an all-day affair in those days. A memorable holiday was spent there with my brother and Gerry Siviour, travelling in his new Ford Prefect, and some of the pictures from this holiday are in the book. Further away, Wales, the North West of England, notably Shap and the Settle & Carlisle line, were places that had to be visited, as well as Scotland of course.

It has been very difficult to know which photographs to include in this book. For every one chosen I have had to put several others aside, sometimes because they did not quite fit in with the themes I have chosen, or they were too avant-garde. However, I trust that you will like this selection, and if so I hope to be able to share some more memories with you in the future. Nearly 37 years have passed since I took the most recent pictures in the book, so my 'memory of the memories' is not as good as it was! Indeed I have only

* *Thanks For The Memory*, words by Leo Robin, music by Ralph Rainger. Copyright 1937 Famous Music Corporation, USA. Used by permission of Music Sales Limited. All Rights Reserved. International Copyright Secured.

recently printed some of the pictures in the book for the first time. In addition, much to my regret, I did not keep the detailed records I should have done when I took the pictures, so have been struggling to ascertain the actual dates for some of them. I have included the date of a photograph where it is known, but hope you will forgive me when this information is not given. Fortunately my younger brother David, who you have seen in the picture on page 6, was rather better than me in keeping records of trips, so he has been a great help to me with dates.

I am also indebted to several friends for assisting with extra information for some of the captions, especially the two 'Johns' – John Edgington, whose knowledge of railways is amazing, and John Gilks – as well as Gerry Siviour, Roger Cruse, Brian Stephenson and John Stretton.

But in the end responsibility for any errors rests with me. My thanks also to Peter Townsend and Will Adams and their colleagues at Silver Link Publishing, for their help in producing this book. There remains one other person who has not only been of great assistance to me, with constructive comment and useful ideas, but who has also cheerfully accepted my passion for railways ever since we met. This is of course my wife Alison, who not only features on page 4, but who also took one of the pictures in the colour section. In the days of steam she became so expert that she could tell the difference in the sound of a 'King' and 'Castle' long before they came into sight. I feel very lucky to have enjoyed her tolerance, interest and encouragement.

Mike Esau, Richmond, Surrey, 2005

Waterloo: rebuilt 'West Country' 4-6-2 No 34008 *Padstow*
Steam-hauled departures from Waterloo often produced striking pictures. On this damp and gloomy winter day the exhaust from *Padstow* makes lovely patterns as the locomotive powers slowly forward under the colour light signal gantry at the end of the platform with the 1.30pm train for Bournemouth.

The power and speed of steam

'Power' and 'speed' are two characteristics forever associated with steam, so I thought it would be appropriate for the pictures in this first section of 'memories' to depict these qualities. Capturing 'power' and 'speed' on camera was not that easy, since a successful picture often involved an element of luck, or being in the right place at the right time.

The proportions alone of a particular class of locomotive could suggest 'Power'. For example, I felt that the unrebuilt 'Merchant Navy' Class (see opposite) possessed this quality, their massive appearance enhanced by the solid-looking air-smoothed casing with which they were clad. When rebuilt, the class were efficient machines, but seemed to have lost the charisma they possessed in their original form. Of the other '8P' 'Pacifics', the 'Princess Coronation' Class looked magnificent even at rest, especially when viewed broadside on.

Panning the camera was an obvious way to show 'Speed', the picture on this page being an example. I found that panning the camera round with the train in conjunction with a shutter speed of 1/100th of a second was about right. The trick was to start panning early before releasing the shutter when the locomotive was directly in front of the camera, but continuing the movement through, all in one flowing swing. If all went well the locomotive would appear slightly off pin sharp, showing just the right degree of movement, but with its wheels and background to the picture nicely blurred to suggest speed.

On other occasions, even though a locomotive was moving fast, there might only be a limited impression of speed or power, perhaps because there was little exhaust from the chimney. Nevertheless, the modest haze of smoke from the chimneys of *Compton Castle* and *Bristol Castle* (pages 10 and 14) suggests that they were travelling at speed, as indeed was the case, but in the understated way of Great Western locomotives when properly driven and fired. In contrast, perhaps because of the type of coal being used, *Lord Rowallan* (page 12) is blacking out the lineside with smoke, giving an impression of both raw power and speed. Moving much more slowly, the 'Crab' at Stainforth on page 15 demonstrates sheer brute force in getting its train on the move – no wonder the line was called 'the Long Drag'.

The penultimate picture in this selection is of a 'V2' 2-6-2, a class that seemed to find it difficult not to give an impression of power once on the move. One of the great sounds of the steam age was the three-cylinder beat of a 'V2' as it was opened up, which changed to that wonderful rhythmic roar once the locomotive took hold of its train. How fortunate we are to have those evocative Peter Handford recordings of this class at work on the 'Waverley Route' in the Scottish Border country.

Rebuilt 'West Country' 4-6-2 No 34044 *Woolacombe* at speed near Esher.

Above **Hither Green: rebuilt 'West Country' 4-6-2 No 34005 *Barnstaple***

In June 1957 No 34005 was the first Bulleid 'light Pacific' to be rebuilt and was allocated to the Eastern Section, where it was allowed to get into an absolutely filthy condition. Nevertheless the locomotive exudes a sense of power as it storms up the 1 in 146 gradient through the station with 'The Man of Kent' bound for Folkestone and Dover. Just look at that wonderful line of tall telegraph poles on the left of the picture.

Right **Folkestone Junction: 'Merchant Navy' 4-6-2 No 35001 *Channel Packet***
The hefty proportions of the 'Merchant Navy' Class in their original condition were impressive, so it was always a thrill to have the chance to photograph one before rebuilding. After coupling up to the stock of this boat train, which has been brought up from the Harbour station, No 35001 is moving out slowly on to the main line for the run up to Victoria.

Adlestrop: 'Castle' 4-6-0 No 5099 *Compton Castle*, 1962
The setting for Edward Thomas's famous poem, the station was still open when this picture was taken. Happily one of the nameboards has been saved and today can be seen in the village. Worcester shed's nicely cleaned 'Castle' is speeding through the station with a train from Paddington to its home city – what a fine sight the locomotive makes.

Above **Chipping Campden Tunnel: '9F' 2-10-0 No 92206**
I was fortunate enough to be issued with a lineside pass by the Western Region covering most of the Oxford to Worcester line, and this facility made all the difference to my photography on this very attractive route. Working powerfully up the 1 in 100 gradient, the Eastleigh-shedded '9F' has just emerged from the south end of the tunnel with a train of empty tankers from Bromford Bridge to Fawley, which are protected by two barrier wagons behind the locomotive.

Right **Birkett Tunnel: '9F' 2-10-0 No 92017, 17 June 1965**
Perhaps working even harder than No 92206, sister locomotive No 92017 bursts out of the tunnel with an anhydrite gypsum train from Long Meg to Widnes, on the long southbound climb to Ais Gill summit on the Settle & Carlisle line.

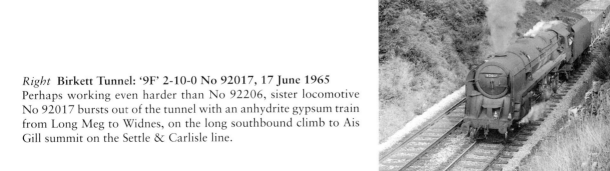

Above **Grayrigg bank: 'Princess Coronation' 4-6-2 No 46230 *Duchess of Buccleuch***
My in-laws lived near Warrington in the days of steam (and happily still do), so I had left their house early in the morning to travel up to Grayrigg and Shap for a day's photography. However, as was often the case the weather conditions worsened as I went north. Although there was an unusual dearth of trains, I did capture this shot of the 'Duchess' forging up the bank in the pouring rain towards a set of catch points, with a northbound working.

Left **Brock troughs: 'Britannia' 4-6-2 No 70045 *Lord Rowallan***
All power and fury and seemingly none the worse for its shocking external condition, the 'Britannia' makes a striking picture on this northbound train passing 'badger bridge' on the main line north of Preston. The driver has worked the locomotive up to a tremendous pace and, perhaps due to what must be lively conditions on the footplate, the fireman has been a little slow in raising the tender scoop. The overflow from the tender is drenching the leading coaches of the train with water.

Dent: '5MT' 4-6-0 No 44983, 18 June 1965
A westerly gale was blowing up Dentdale, so I had to brace myself against the bridge parapet to hold the camera steady in order to photograph this northbound train of coal empties. Nevertheless, the poor weather conditions have I feel added to the appeal of the picture. In those days it was very rare to meet any other photographers along the line, especially at a remote place like Dent – certainly the day I took this picture was no exception.

Above **Near Charlbury: 'Castle' 4-6-0 No 7013 *Bristol Castle*, July 1962**
A charming and neat permanent way hut sets off this picture of the 'Castle' speeding towards Oxford with a train from Worcester. The feather of steam from the safety valve bonnet shows that the fireman has done his job well.

Left **South of Haddenham: 'V2' 2-6-2 No 60866, 11 March 1961**
On one of my regular visits to the Paddington-Birmingham line to photograph the 'King' Class, the day was enlivened by this special train to Wembley for a schoolgirl hockey final. I feel sure that I was enjoying the sound of the Doncaster-based 'V2' as it accelerated its train towards the capital.

Stainforth: '5MT' 'Crab' 2-6-0 No 42907
The 'Waverley' express has just passed me on its northbound journey, clearing the way for the 'Crab' to start the slow climb to Ais Gill summit. I remember that the locomotive was making an all-out effort to get its heavy train on the move up the 1 in 100 gradient.

Beginnings and endings

The terminus station has a special place in my memories, for here you could enjoy the spectacle of the departure of a prestigious main-line train or contemplate the finer points of the design of a locomotive as it rested at the buffer stops after a long journey from some distant city. Living close to London I was able to visit all the London termini, so several of them appear in this section. Some offered more to the photographer than others, especially the old Euston and nearby St Pancras. Euston was full of contrasts, from its long gloomy platforms to the elegance of the Great Hall hidden in the heart of the station. It is inconceivable today that a structure as striking as the Great Hall could have been demolished during the rebuilding of the station. The huge arched roof of St. Pancras provided an unrivalled setting for photographing steam, but the lighting was difficult because of the station's north aspect. However, I was lucky when I photographed the 'Waverley' express arriving one summer evening (page 21).

I always looked forward to the approach to Euston, down the bank past Camden shed, where there would nearly always be a glimpse of a huge 'Princess Coronation' 'Pacific' waiting for its next turn of duty. On my way home, the Northern Line would take me to Waterloo. Coming up the escalator into the station, the all-over glass roof and the wide concourse gave an overwhelming feeling of light and space, a total contrast to the sooty but lovable old Euston. From a photographic point of view Waterloo came into its own in the late afternoon as the sun moved round to the ideal position for photographing evening departures to the west, such as the 5.43pm to Salisbury (page 17).

Once the sun had set there was always the chance for some night photography, so I have included two pictures taken after dark at Norwich Thorpe and Marylebone (page 25). I rarely used flash since I think the harsh results looked unnatural, and the sudden bursts of light could be distracting for railway staff. Provided you were under cover, a rainy night produced the best results, with the station lights reflected on the wet platforms.

Outside London, during railway holidays in the late 1950s, I was able to take photographs of the terminal stations at opposite ends of the country at Penzance and Thurso. Both stations possessed all-over roofs, although the one at Thurso was modest in comparison with Penzance (page 24). On a smaller scale, photography at a country branch terminus was invariably rewarding – often an adjacent single-road locomotive shed and goods yard could be included in the picture. But this section of pictures is really about main-line stations, so I have included some smaller termini, such as Ashburton and Wallingford, elsewhere in the book.

'Princess Coronation' 4-6-2 No 46229 *Duchess of Hamilton* after arrival at platform 6 in Euston.

Above **London Bridge: '4MT' 2-6-4T No 42087 and 2-BIL EMU**
Compared to the cramped layout of the Eastern Section station at
London Bridge, the terminal Central Section side was very
spacious. This shows up well in this picture of an Oxted line train
waiting to leave during the off-peak period when the station
assumed an air of calm unknown today.

Below **Waterloo: 'Battle of Britain' 4-6-2 No 34089 *602 Squadron***
I much appreciated having a Southern Region lineside
photographic pass, but it was not valid in third-rail areas. This
meant that it was not possible to obtain a picture of a train leaving
Waterloo from track level with the station in the background.
However, by catching a train on the Windsor side that departed
about the same time as the 5.43pm to Salisbury, I was lucky
enough to obtain this pleasing shot of the train.

Left **King's Cross: 'A4' 4-6-2 No 60026 *Miles Beevor***
Working in central London quite near to King's Cross and Euston, I was sometimes able to take a picture or two during my lunch break. On this cold winter day, the 'A4' is in charge of the 1.15pm train to Leeds. As often happened when the locomotive's regulator was first opened on starting, the driving wheels are slipping. One of the station staff has just put out some food for the birds, which have been startled by the spectacular and noisy eruption from the locomotive. Nevertheless they add to the picture – what a pity the 'A4' was not No 60033 *Seagull*!

Above **Paddington: 'Castle' 4-6-0 No 7007 *Great Western***
Being hemmed in by tall buildings, there never seemed to be much direct sunlight to photograph departures from Paddington. Nevertheless some lovely pictures were to be had, particularly suited to black and white film. Nicely cleaned, with burnished front buffers, No 7007 makes a superb subject for my camera as it waits impatiently to depart with what is I think is the 1.15pm train to Worcester. The locomotive proudly carries the distinctive GWR coat of arms on the middle driving wheel splasher.

Right **Paddington: 'King' 4-6-0 No 6022 *King Edward III***
On a rather murky day, so typical of the age of working steam, the fireman checks the road as the 'King' moves forward out of the station with a train for Birmingham Snow Hill, Chester and Birkenhead.

Above **St Pancras: rebuilt 'Royal Scot' 4-6-0, 'Jubilee' 4-6-0 No 45566 *Queensland*, and '4MT' 2-6-4T**

Sandwiched between Euston and King's Cross, St Pancras did not offer the opportunity to photograph glamorous '8P' locomotives such as 'Princess Coronations' and 'A4s'. However, I was fortunate to be able to capture this trio, a rebuilt 'Scot' waiting to run light to Kentish Town shed, the 'Jubilee' pulling out on an express for Leicester, and the '4MT' on station pilot duties.

Below **Manchester Central: '4MT' 2-6-4T No 42455**

Set off by the huge clock, the station's roof span of 210 feet is almost as impressive as its St Pancras counterpart and provides a fine setting for this picture of Trafford Park's No 42455 waiting to leave platform 2 with a train for the Warrington and Liverpool line.

Above **St Pancras: '2P' 4-4-0 No 40491 and 'Jubilee' 4-6-0, 1958**
Central London was sweltering on this hot summer evening. I had come into the shade of St Pancras station from Euston Road to see the arrival of the up 'Waverley' due in at around 8pm. The pilot locomotive is a Leeds Holbeck 1912-built '2P' 4-4-0 with 7ft 0½in driving wheels, amazingly still in front-line service. At this time in the summer, the evening sun illuminates the interior of the train shed and is highlighting the oil that has spun out along the spokes of the front bogie wheels of the '2P'. Quite probably the old 4-4-0 was hustled along by the 'Jubilee', giving its crew quite a lively ride. Sustained by full dining car facilities, what scenic delights those passengers travelling from Edinburgh would have experienced during the course of their journey south – the bleak hills of the 'Waverley Route' around Stobs and Whitrope and the breezy moorland over the Settle & Carlisle line. Oh, that we could make such a journey again today!

Euston: '8P' 4-6-2 No 71000 *Duke of Gloucester* and 'Princess Coronation' 4-6-2 No 46225 *Duchess of Gloucester*

It was a stroke of luck to find this noble couple waiting to leave Euston with lunchtime trains for Scotland – the 'Duke' at platform 12 is on the 1.35pm to Perth, the 'Duchess' at platform 13 on the 'Midday Scot'. I wonder if any fellow photographers captured the two locomotives standing side by side on some other occasion. It is interesting to compare the designs of the two 'Pacifics', but to my eye the 'Duchess' looks better proportioned and more businesslike.

Right **Liverpool Street: 'N7' 0-6-2T, 29 October 1960**
Here is Liverpool Street station as it was very often seen, blurred by smoke and steam. Under the delicate tracery of the station roof on platform 2, a porter is loading mailbags, while on the other platform haphazard piles of luggage and parcels await attention. What a wonderful steam-age atmosphere, although this would all become a memory the following month when electric services commenced on the suburban lines out of Liverpool Street.

Below **Victoria: 'H' 0-4-4T**
'A foggy day in London Town…' Standing out against the lighter background, the 'H' in platform 2 has just brought in the empty stock of a departure to the Kent coast. The evocative sign behind the train proclaims that the 'Night Ferry' is still running. This left the terminus at 9pm or 10pm according to the time of year.

Below **Penzance: 'Castle' 4-6-0 No 5058 *Earl of Clancarty*, September 1958**
Here I am down in far Penzance, 305¼ miles from Paddington, during a railway tour of the West Country. The 'Castle' has brought in its train of smart Mk I coaches from Plymouth and is easing them back to enable it to reach the points, so that it can run round to proceed to the shed for servicing.

Bottom **Thurso: '3MT' 2-6-2T, July 1959**
Another railway holiday, this time to Scotland, afforded me the strange experience of being able to take daylight photographs at Wick as late as 10pm. Rather earlier in the day, the Stanier tank has just arrived at the overall-roofed station from Georgemas Junction with its train of two ex-LMS coaches. It has been met by some local boys and a Post Office van. The distance by rail from Penzance to Thurso, according to the route taken, is some 950 miles.

Right **Norwich Thorpe: 'J15' 0-6-0 No 65469, 'M&GN Special', 8 October 1960**
Although I did not do much night photography in steam days, the two pictures on this page were taken when the conditions seemed right. Norwich shed's 'J15' makes a very pleasant sight on this wet evening at Thorpe Station. Happily one of the Lowestoft 'J15s', No 65462, survived, and is based at the North Norfolk Railway.

Below right **Marylebone: Standard '5MT' 4-6-0 No 73066, 'The South Yorkshireman', 2 January 1960**
I have rested my camera on the barrier at the end of the platform to capture this rather sad image of the last up 'South Yorkshireman', the day that marked the end of through workings to and from Manchester and Sheffield. This train first appeared in the timetable in 1948. No attempt has been made to provide a clean locomotive. Once the empty stock backs out into the darkness this named train will be just a memory, a precursor to the slow run-down of the old Great Central Railway route into London.

Travellers and railwaymen

*I*n the steam era, such was the attraction of the locomotive that few railway photographers seemed interested enough to take pictures of travellers and railwaymen in their own right. There are some excellent official collections of railway staff at work, but few informal photographs. I was always on the lookout for pictures of people on the railway, although I would never ask anyone to pose for a picture, which would invariably give an unnatural result. It was in any case quite difficult to get to know railwaymen in those days, so really the best approach was to be prepared for 'photo opportunities', to use that awful modern expression.

The small eye-level viewfinder on the medium-format roll-film camera equipment I used for most of the steam era was not ideal for spontaneous pictures of people, but I managed as best I could. What was really needed was a compact 35mm SLR camera or, better still, a Rollei twin lens reflex, with its big viewfinder screen, standard issue for the press photographers of the day. Unfortunately, though, the cost of a Rolleiflex was more than I could afford at the time. However, salvation did arrive in the form of the Bronica S single lens reflex camera, which I won in a *Weekend Telegraph* colour supplement photographic competition in the mid-1960s. The big screen made picture composition easy, although when the shutter was released and the mirror flew up, the noise was hardly unobtrusive! In fact, only three of the pictures in this section were taken with this camera, on page 28 (upper) and both on page 34, so my Zeiss Ikon and Voightlanders couldn't have been that bad for this sort of photography.

Apart from the railway staff and the travellers, in those more leisurely days, there were the enthusiasts who thronged the railway in the steam era, notably the 'spotters' collecting loco numbers from the ends of platforms at stations and at other good viewpoints, all over the country. How can I forget the up and down West Coast Main Line platforms at Preston station in the early 1950s, where large numbers of schoolboys would congregate, rushing en masse from one side to the other with excited shouts of 'Streak!' or 'Namer!'. The station staff must have been very tolerant in those days. Though much fewer in number to those found at Preston, I have included photographs of enthusiasts at Basingstoke (page 33) and a favourite picture taken at Oxenholme one wet day, as two lads watch the departure of a northbound freight. You will also find a rather nice picture of enthusiasts at the top of page 123 in the 'Special Trains' section. Just like the travellers depicted on page 34, how well turned out they look.

At Bournemouth Central my son Richard admires rebuilt 'West Country' 4-6-2 No 34001 *Exeter* through the window of a Bulleid coach.

Newton Heath shed, Manchester: '5MT' 4-6-0 No 45025
On this rather damp day, the well-turned-out Class '5' is being prepared for its next turn of duty. The 1934-built locomotive was in service right up to the end of steam on British Railways in 1968, and was one of the lucky ones of the class to be preserved; it is currently based on the Strathspey Railway.

Left **Waterloo**

As a change from photographing enginemen, it was good to obtain this picture of two fitters making an essential repair to what looks like a split water column hose. The wooden ladder is being held firmly in place by the lower man, while another member of staff is keeping a lookout. In the background are a Standard Class '3' 2-6-2T, a glimpse of a Bulleid rebuilt 'Pacific' and a 2-BIL EMU leaving for Reading.

Below **Waterloo: 'King Arthur' 4-6-0 No 30748 *Vivien***

The fireman is topping up the big double bogie tender with water, very important since the locomotive could be standing at the buffer stops for some time awaiting release. Do notice the second water column for the use of locomotives coming in tender-first and the sign advertising 6d admission to Battersea Fun Fair.

Opposite **Culmstock: '1400' 0-4-2T No 1440, April 1960**
Brill & Ludgershall: '6400' 0-6-0PT No 6403, 4 March 1961

These pictures are a reminder of the more leisurely age of steam when sometimes there was time to spare. Certain workings on the 7½-mile Tiverton Junction-Hemyock branch only ran as far as Uffculme or Culmstock. No 1440 has run round its single ex-Barry Railway gas-lit coach at Culmstock ready to return to the main line, allowing the train crew a few minutes to look at the small station garden.

At deserted Brill & Ludgershall station No 6403, working a Princes Risborough to Banbury auto-train, is waiting for a Birmingham train to pass on the through road. The driver is chatting to the guard by the front driving compartment of the coach, while the fireman looks on from the cab of the Pannier tank.

This page **Brading: 'O2' 0-4-2T No W35** *Freshwater*
Mill Hill: train from Cowes to Ryde Pier Head
Visits to the unique Isle of Wight railway system in steam days would invariably produce some valued pictures. On the busy Ryde to Shanklin section the signalman is preparing to take the token from the fireman of No W35 so the other train can proceed on the single-line section to Smallbrook Junction.

At Mill Hill station the guard is picked out by steam billowing from the 208-yard-long Cowes Tunnel as he prepares to give the train the 'right away' for Newport.

Opposite **Horsmonden: 'C' 0-6-0 No 31244**
Medstead & Four Marks: '700' 0-6-0 No 30325, 29 August 1957
No 31244 has uncoupled from its short pick-up goods train at Horsmonden on the Hawkhurst branch The guard has the key to unlock the ground frame, which will enable the very dirty 'C' to enter the goods yard. Do notice the coal merchant's lorry on the extreme right of the picture, the two Ford cars and the oast-houses.

On the Alton to Winchester Junction line (part of which forms the modern 'Mid-Hants Railway') the guard has time to contemplate the inner workings of the old '700' while waiting to pass an up train from Winchester. The driver's attire could be a model for MHR footplate staff wishing to look authentic!

Above **Oxenholme: '4MT' 2-6-4T No 42571**
On the same occasion as the picture at the top of page 12, I have called in at Oxenholme station to see what photographs might be on offer, and not least to try and dry out a little! I am in luck as a northbound fitted freight train has just trundled into the station and stopped to take on a banker in the form of the Stanier tank, for the climb up Grayrigg. Two young lads, one well protected from the wet in a sou'wester and Wellington boots, have braved the rain to watch the spectacle of the heavy freight getting away from the station up the 1 in 178 gradient towards the fells.

Opposite **Basingstoke: '4MT' 4-6-0 No 75066**
Basingstoke: rebuilt 'Merchant Navy' 4-6-2 No 35013 *United States Lines*
More Wellington boots for another wet day – at the west end of the station the driver of No 75066 is carefully reversing his locomotive to couple up to a summer Saturday train from the London Midland Region. The plates on the back of the businesslike-looking tender show that it is a BR1B type, No 1030, holding 7 tons of coal and 4,725 gallons of water.

The other picture was also taken at the west end of the station where No 35013 is taking water and will shortly leave with a train for Bournemouth. As you can see, duffle-bags were very popular in the 1960s.

Opposite **Bournemouth**
Waterloo: the 'Bournemouth Belle'
I sometimes found the passengers as interesting as the trains. How smart everybody looks in this picture taken on the up platform at Bournemouth as a Standard Class '4' brings in a train from Weymouth. What a remarkable trio of hats those ladies on the left are wearing! Maybe everybody had been to a wedding.

Meanwhile, at Waterloo passengers in the 'Bournemouth Belle' Pullman car are settling down for their 2-hour journey to Bournemouth. The *Daily Sketch* the lady passenger is holding carries a headline about 'Boom Pilots', possibly in connection the then growing nuisance of sonic booms from fast-flying jet aircraft, though the first test flights of Concorde were not made until a few years after I took this picture.

Above **Sandown, 1964**
In the days before the majority of holidaymakers went on holiday by car, a packed train has just arrived at Sandown station on the Isle of Wight. The train is one of the frequent summer Saturday services from Ryde Pier Head, hauled by an 'O2' 0-4-4T. To our

21st-century eyes this scene has many interesting features, such as the antiquated pre-Grouping rolling-stock and the smartly dressed passengers. Unless there were porters around, it was hard work carrying your luggage in those days – the widespread use of wheeled cases with a towing handle was still in the future.

Steam in the seasons

The seasons of the year have a profound influence on railway photography, not only through climatic factors, but also because of the pattern of train services. Although there were more trains to photograph in the late spring and summer months of the year as the holiday season got under way, the strong light and high temperatures prevented any striking exhaust effects. The seasonal effect on train services was more marked on some lines than others. The Somerset and Dorset (S&D) came into its own in the summer months with a procession of holiday trains to and from the Midlands and North to the South West on Saturdays. Famous among these was the Cleethorpes to Exmouth train, which in 1962 ran on Saturdays between 28 July and 1 September. The southbound train left the East Coast resort at 7am, eventually arriving in Exmouth via Sidmouth Junction nearly 11 hours later at 5.40pm. What a marathon journey!

Naturally the S&D was the place to go on Summer Saturdays, particularly since it offered the chance to photograph exotic combinations of motive power like an S&D 2-8-0 piloted by a '2P' 4-4-0, or the '4F' and unrebuilt Bulleid 'Pacific' seen on page 38. Almost any main line at summer weekends would produce a rich crop of extra workings, some inter-regional, like the 'Schools' opposite. Such interesting trains made up for the hot weather conditions.

As summer faded, I looked forward not only to the autumnal colours in the trees along the line, but also to the seasonal freight traffic. For example, Midhurst on the Southern Region was a centre for sugar beet traffic. There were the hop-pickers' trains too, although these were rapidly declining in the late 1950s, coming to an end in 1960. Flooding of the line because of heavy autumnal rain could produce some interesting workings, as I show on page 44.

Just as now, the best conditions for railway photography were often in the winter when the sun was lower in the sky and temperatures dropped. There was always the promise of snow and that came with a vengeance during the memorable winter of 1962/63. We had travelled up to my in-laws in Warrington for Christmas on the Lambretta, but so bad did the weather become while we were there that I had to put the scooter on the train for our return to London. Even the road journey back from Euston to our bedsitter in Putney was challenging. Some of the pictures I took during this hard winter are included in this section.

Spring, too, was a great time to be out with a camera. The holiday I spent with my brother and Gerry Siviour in the West Country in April 1960 was outstanding, not only because of the range of locomotives we were able to photograph, but also because of the clear Spring light during that sunny week. This was the last time the elegant 'T9' 4-4-0s could be seen regularly at work on the North Cornwall lines to Padstow and Bude, and I also photographed No 30715 working the Plymouth portion of the 'Atlantic Coast Express' near Lydford. With Beattie 'Well tanks' still in charge of the Wadebridge to Wenford Bridge goods trains, as well as classic Great Western motive power a few miles away on the Devon and Cornwall branches and the main line to Penzance, what more could you ask for?

Alison is sitting on our Lambretta TV 175 Series II scooter, 63 XPF, watching '9F' No 92001 coming south near Masbury with an S&D summer Saturday train in 1962.

Summer

Above **Between Edenbridge and Godstone: 'Schools' 4-4-0 No 30917 *Ardingly***
The neat rows of corn stooks in the field adjacent to the line show that this is late summer. The 'Schools' is en route to Redhill and thence to Reading via Guildford with a train for the Western Region.

Below **Near Berkhamsted: unrebuilt 'Patriot' 4-6-0, 1959**
The strong summer light of this hot and hazy summer afternoon emphasises the unmistakable chunky outline of this unrebuilt 'Patriot' It is hauling a train composed of ex-LMS stock, which makes a pleasing picture heading south past newly mown fields towards Euston.

Above **Chilcompton Tunnel: '4F' 0-6-0 No 44102 and unrebuilt 'West Country' 4-6-2 No 34043 *Combe Martin***

On summer weekends in the early 1960s a regular trip was down the A30/A303 from my home in New Malden to visit the Somerset & Dorset line. Alison and I travelled on our Lambretta scooter, seen on page 36, and, allowing for a comfortable top cruising speed of around 50mph, could be in Wincanton to start photographing around mid-morning. Of course in those days the route west was quiet compared to now and suited to our modest form of transport. Because of the north-to-south alignment of the S&D, trains from Bournemouth were coming out of the sun for several hours on a fine day, so I tended to concentrate on the southbound workings. Working hard up the 1 in 50 gradient, this splendid combination has just burst out of Chilcompton Tunnel on the climb from Radstock.

Above right **Between Corfe Castle and Swanage: 'M7' 0-4-4T No 30107 and unrebuilt 'West Country' 4-6-2 No 34093 *Saunton*, 1961**

Summer Saturdays saw through trains between Waterloo and Swanage, sometimes piloted by one of Bournemouth shed's 'M7s' as an assisting locomotive on the branch line. I am sure the 'Pacific' could have managed this train quite easily by itself, but perhaps the 'M7' was tacked on the front to avoid a light engine movement back to Swanage. On this hot day the train, formed of Bulleid coaches, is about to go under the main road from Wareham to Swanage. Corfe Castle stands proud on the horizon.

Right **Talerddig summit: Standard '4MT' 4-6-0s**

From Machynlleth to Talerddig there is an almost continuous climb of some 15 miles at a ruling gradient of 1 in 52. This formidable ascent made double-heading essential for heavy Summer Saturday holiday trains, and consequently the area was a magnet for railway photographers. I was no exception, and here we have the fine sight of no fewer than four Standard Class '4s' crossing at the top of the climb. The two locomotives nearest the camera arrived first, while the other two are coming in from the Shrewsbury direction.

Between Wolvercote Junction and Handborough: 'Castle' 4-6-0 No 7027 *Thornbury Castle*, 1962

What can I say about this picture of a Paddington to Worcester train taken on a perfect English early summer day? The hawthorn blossom is out, the sky is filled with lovely white cumulus clouds and all feels right with the world.

Old Basing: Standard '5MT' 4-6-0

On this summer morning I have come up into the churchyard to photograph the Standard Class '5' on the eastern outskirts of Basingstoke. Do you remember 'VG Foodstores'? Note also the now old-fashioned high pram with its sunshade canopy in front of the shop.

Autumn

Opposite top **Bodiam: 'A1X' 0-6-0T No 32678,
2 September 1957**
One of the highlights for the railway photographer in the autumn was the coming of the hop-picking season and the special trains this produced. I have travelled down to Kent to see this 'hop-pickers' friends' train, which was worked over the former Kent & East Sussex Railway section from Robertsbridge by two 'Terriers', one at each end of the coaches. In the event I was almost the only passenger back to London on this sultry evening. The staff chat on the small weed-grown platform before the train returns to the main line.

Opposite below **Cranbrook: 'C' 0-6-0 No 31293,
13 September 1959**
The 'H84' number carried on the front of the locomotive shows this to be another 'hop-pickers' friends' train, which Gerry Siviour and I have come specially to photograph. This was the last such working on the Hawkhurst branch. The driver of the old Bricklayers Arms shed 'C' told us that he had to take the train through to London and would have to tackle the climb through Hildenborough and up to Polhill once on the main line.

Above **Between Petworth and Fittleworth: 'E4' 0-6-2T
No 32469, 19 November 1960**
On this glorious clear autumn day, the low sun has picked out every detail of the 'E4' heading this goods train from Midhurst to Horsham. Apart from the covered van, the train consists of wagons filled with sugar beet loaded at Midhurst en route for refining at a factory at Allscott, between Wellington and Shrewsbury in Shropshire. Although the line closed to passenger traffic in 1955, the track looks well cared for.

Left **Allbrook: rebuilt 'Bulleid' 4-6-2**
Late-autumn rains have swollen the River Itchen between Shawford and Eastleigh, which is the setting for this picture of a down train heading for Southampton. The last time I visited this location, a clear view of the line was prevented by the unchecked growth of trees and bushes.

Below left **Southerham Junction, Lewes: 'K' 2-6-0 No 32341, 5 November 1960**
Especially after heavy autumnal rain, the River Ouse at Lewes was prone to bursting its banks and flooding the line. In early November 1960 the situation was especially severe, so normal electric services had to be suspended. To cope with the situation Brighton shed has turned out its nicely cleaned 'K' Class 'Mogul' to haul a three-coach Maunsell set, which provides a service along the coast towards Hastings. A half-hourly service was maintained along the coast route, worked by a variety of motive power. Today, I suspect, the line would be closed and a bus service substituted!

Winter

Right **Hayling Island: 'A1X' 0-6-0 No 32650**
The sort of weather conditions greeting No 32650 as it bustles into the station from Havant are well portrayed in black and white. The wet platform, glistening rails and 'drooping' gas lamp all add to the atmosphere of this scene.

Below **Marlow: '1400' 0-4-2T No 1474, 21 January 1961**
Another wet platform, another dismal day. No 1474 blows off steam as it waits impatiently to leave for the 2¾-mile run to Bourne End with its push-and-pull train, popularly known as the 'Marlow Donkey'.

Above **Chilworth: 'S15' 4-6-0 No 30835, January 1963**
During the very hard winter of 1962/63 Alison and I have braved the snowy roads on the Lambretta to take some pictures along the Guildford to Redhill line. I remember that we kept stepping into hidden rabbit holes as we struggled along the embankment in the deep snow. The 'S15' was having an equally difficult time keeping its long freight train on the move up the 1 in 100 gradient towards Gomshall, so much so that we were able to photograph it again before it reached the summit of the climb.

Above right **Between Chilworth and Gomshall: 'U' 2-6-0 No 31796, January 1963**
On the same day this 'U' Class locomotive makes a fine sight with a short train for Redhill. Despite a north wind, which could have blown the steam over the train, the exhaust from the locomotive has lifted just enough to clear the last coach.

Right **Rowfant: 'M7' 0-4-4T No 30053, 23 February 1963**
Rowfant was one of my favourite stations, a very quiet spot tucked away in the woods between Three Bridges and East Grinstead. The little station building on the eastbound side was a delight with its steep pitched roof – at the time of a recent visit the building was still there. On the westbound platform some local lads are enjoying the snow before it melts as the 'M7' pauses at the station with a push-and-pull train to the main line at Three Bridges.

Above **Warrington Arpley: '3F' 0-6-0T No 47657, December 1962**

On a freezing cold day, the 'Jinty' is taking water in the massive yard. The Thames Board Mills are to the left and in the background on the right a freight train can be seen drifting down towards Bank Quay station on the West Coast Main Line.

Below **Winwick: '5MT' 4-6-0**

Forty or so years ago the land to the north of Warrington was open fields and had not yet been built on. The flat open landscape, together with the north-to-south alignment of the West Coast Main Line, provided the right conditions to obtain some nice back-lit photographs of northbound trains such as this one of a Class '5' on a freight heading towards Wigan.

Spring

Above **Saunderton: 'WD' '8F' 2-8-0**
In my opinion, Saunderton bank was one of the best photographic locations on any of the northbound main-line routes out of London in the days of working steam. The double track ran through a wide gap in the Chilterns, which provided many good positions, including a section at the top of the climb where the up and down lines separated for a short distance. On a bright cold day early in spring, the 2-8-0 is making steady progress up the 1 in 164 gradient towards the station with an enormous haul of coal empties. In contrast to the overgrown condition of the lineside today, the well-trimmed bank has enabled me to capture the full length of this impressive train.

Right **Shepton Mallet (Charlton Road): '4MT' 2-6-4T No 80147, 3 April 1965**
The months of March and April can produce some of the best conditions for railway photography. The light has an intense clear quality that is lost as the sun climbs higher in the sky with the approach of summer and rising temperatures. On this fine Spring day No 80147 pulls away from Shepton Mallet with a local train from Bath Green Park to Evercreech Junction.

Left **Lydford (Western Region): '4500' 2-6-2T No 5569, April 1960**
As I have already related, Gerry Siviour, my brother and I spent a wonderful week in the West Country in April 1960 when the sun never seemed to stop shining. In the course of photographing 'T9s' on the Southern lines, we visited Lydford on the northern flank of Dartmoor. The Western Region station can be seen in the background as the 2-6-2T leaves with one of the infrequent trains for Plymouth North Road. In the foreground is the track connecting the Southern and Western Region lines put in during the Second World War.

Below **Gara Bridge: '4500' 2-6-2T No 4561, April 1960**
Equally as delightful as Lydford, but set in the lush valley of the River Avon, Gara Bridge station is in the background of this picture of No 4561 pulling out for Kingsbridge. Two camping coaches can be seen behind the ex-LNER van bringing up the rear of the train.

Right **Between Ashurst and Groombridge: '2MT' 2-6-2T No 41326**
The embankments of the rural lines in Sussex always seemed to provide a wonderful display of flowers in the spring. Cowslips and primroses are in abundance as this Ivatt tank makes its way south en route for Tunbridge Wells West with a train from Oxted.

Below **Between Cranbrook and Goudhurst: 'C' 0-6-0 No 31716**
I love the breezy wide open feel of this picture showing the 'C' coasting down the bank toward Goudhurst with a pick-up goods from Hawkhurst. In the background the washing is blowing merrily on the line while a young mother pushes a tall old-fashioned black pram through the garden.

Steam around Britain

That this is the largest section of 'memories' is not surprising, since I was lucky enough to be able to travel almost everywhere in the British Isles where steam was still at work. Unfortunately, because steam went comparatively early in East Anglia and the East of England I was only able to take a few pictures in these areas, and for some reason I also never visited the south-west of Scotland; perhaps I was in a hurry to get to the scenically superior Highlands to the north. The pictures in this section are arranged to start in the South East, thence to the West Country and Wales, on to the North and North West of England, then finally to Scotland.

I don't think I favoured one area above all others since everywhere had its particular qualities and attractions, so I was just happy to be out with my camera. As I have hinted in the Introduction, if I had to list outstanding locations I suppose the North Cornwall lines west of Okehampton, the Cambrian Coast line between Dovey Junction and Porthmadog, the Settle & Carlisle line, the 'Waverley Route' and the West Highland line between Fort William and Mallaig would be in my '1st Division'. Needless to say, all these lines are represented in the selection of pictures here.

I can't mention the West Highland line without recalling the epic journey my brother and I made to it from our home in New Malden in the summer of 1961. Lambretta scooters seem to feature large in this book, but it was on my then new LI 125 that we set out for far Mallaig – such was our faith in the machine that we didn't even have a spare wheel.

In fact, no mechanical trouble of any description occurred during the whole journey, which must have amounted to some 1,200 miles. However, as I relate in the captions to the pictures on pages 94 and 99, trouble came in other forms like camera failure and the wet weather that was waiting for us on the West Highland line.

These outstanding lines apart, the South East offered a wide variety of motive power to photograph, notably on the Southern Region. Where else could you readily photograph pre-Grouping classes at work on a day-to-day basis, even into the early 1960s? Outside the Southern Region there were still gems to see like the 'C13s' and 'F5s' on the Chesham and Ongar branches (pages 54 and 55), while into East Anglia there were outposts of interesting steam at Cambridge and Norwich. The latter provided the motive power for the celebrated North Elmham milk train depicted on page 91, one of the last steam workings in the area.

Much further north was the last bastion of intensive steam working in the North East centred around the colliery lines at Blyth and Ashington – what a different world from the cosseted South East this was! Today, looking at the pictures taken on these mineral lines, I can't believe just how few other cars there were on the adjacent roads.

I hope you enjoy this selection of 'Steam around Britain', which not only shows the diverse characteristics of the country the railways ran through, but also the rich variety of locomotives and trains that could be enjoyed.

Steam in the British landscape – '4MT' 2-6-4T No 80132 heads down the valley of the River Dovey between Cemmes Road and Machynlleth with a local train from Shrewsbury.

Above **Grove Junction, Tunbridge Wells: 'C' 0-6-0 No 31588**
Tonbridge shed must have been stretched for suitable motive power, as it has turned out its woebegone-looking 'C' to work this stopping train to Hastings. The train has just emerged from the 287-yard-long Grove Tunnel to pass the signal box controlling the junction with the Tunbridge Wells West line.

Below **Between Dunton Green and Chevening Halt: 'H' 0-4-4T No 31193**
I remember that snow was threatening when I took this picture of the 'H' not long after it had left the main line at Dunton Green bound for Westerham hauling the two delightful coaches converted from SE&CR steam railmotors. The M25 now runs along the alignment of the branch in this area.

Above **Roydon: 'N7' 0-6-2T, 12 November 1960**
Located between Broxbourne and Harlow, the station's pleasing little signal box and level crossing provide the setting for this picture of a train for Bishop's Stortford, just prior to the electrification of the Liverpool Street suburban lines (see page 23).

Left **Between North Weald and Epping: 'F5' 2-4-2T No 67202**
I had travelled into Essex by Underground to ride on and photograph the steam-hauled trains on the Epping to Ongar line shortly before it was electrified on 18 November 1957. Despite its comparative proximity to London, this line was very rural in nature, as shown in this picture of the wheezy old 'F5' with its lightweight train.

Right **Between Chesham and Chalfont & Latimer: 'C13' 4-4-2T No 67420, 26 July 1958**
Vintage stock was also to be found on this delightful line on the southern slopes of the Chilterns. Working hard round one of the many curves on this steeply graded branch, the push-and-pull-fitted 'C13', from Neasden shed, is hauling a train of ex-Metropolitan Railway 'Ashbury' stock towards the main line at Chalfont. The 'Ashbury' coaches have been saved and are in use at the Bluebell Railway.

Below **Watlington: '5700' 0-6-0PT No 4650, 29 June 1957**
My National Service in the RAF had just been completed so I was feeling very happy and relaxed for this visit to the Watlington branch on its last day of operation. The Pannier tank has arrived at the small terminus from Princes Risborough with its single-coach train. As you can guess from the attire of the few people on the platform, the day was a very hot one with the temperature in the 80s.

Above Wallingford: '1400' 0-4-4T No 1447, 1958
Looking rather lost at the end of the long single platform, No 1447 waits to leave on the 2¾-mile journey to Cholsey & Moulsford in the summer of 1958. The station has a sad air of neglect about it, with the single-road engine shed out of use on the left of the picture.

Below Bledlow: '6100' 2-6-2T No 6142, 4 March 1961
On this bright Spring morning, No 6142 leaves the station bound for Oxford with a train from Princes Risborough. With the main line to Birmingham (Snow Hill) a mile or two away, I would have spent much of the rest of the day photographing 'Kings'. Usually when we were in the area, Alison and I would visit Thame to buy delicious freshly baked pasties and lardy cakes for our lunch.

Above **Newbury: 'Castle' 4-6-0, 'Hall' 4-6-0 No 6923 *Croxteth Hall*, and 'T9' 4-4-0 No 30313**
At the east end of the station, the 'T9' is waiting to leave the bay platform with a train for Didcot, while to the left a 'Castle', on an up express to Paddington, is passing the 'Hall' working a stopping train to Reading.

Below **Thame: '6100' 2-6-2Ts Nos 6111 and 6156**
The overall Brunel roof of Thame station was especially attractive, and I always admired the station's fine collection of gas lamps, a few of which can be seen in this picture. No 6111 is taking water at the up platform while No 6156 arrives with a train from Princes Risborough.

Above **Wickham: 'U' 2-6-0 No 31637, 1958**
The Meon Valley line was one of those legendary routes in the South of England running through delightful countryside, which many enthusiasts had heard of but few travelled on. In the early 1950s there were only four trains in each direction on Monday to Saturday and none on Sundays. Passenger services were withdrawn in February 1955, but freight carried on until 30 April 1962. Much of the track had already been lifted by the time I took this picture; on its way to Droxford, by then the northern extremity of the line, No 31637 is shunting some wagons in the long siding on the up side.

Left **Easton: '5700' 0-6-0PT No 8799, May 1958**
I attended a geography field course in Weymouth and, as part of my work project, arranged to travel on the freight train to the Isle of Portland to study the transport of Portland stone from the quarries. The Pannier tank has just arrived at Easton and will return to Weymouth after picking up some wagons loaded with blocks of the stone.

Right **Langston Bridge: 'A1X' 0-6-0T No 32677**
Langston Bridge was very picturesque and provided a wonderful setting in which to photograph the frequent trains on the Hayling Island branch. Before the introduction of more modern rolling-stock, the 'Terrier' makes a splendid picture hauling the two ex-LSWR coaches on a train from Havant.

Below **Ryde Pier: 'O2' 0-4-4T No W24** *Calbourne*
Tantalising puffs of white steam from an 'O2' as the Portsmouth ferry approached Ryde Pier Head station were usually the first hints of the delights awaiting the railway photographer on the Isle of Wight. If travelling only as far as Ryde, one of the clattery old Drewry railcars would save a walk along the pier to the esplanade. On a fine summer evening the railcar is approaching Ryde Esplanade station as the 'O2' pulls out with a train for the Pier Head.

Between Teignmouth and Dawlish: 'Castle' 4-6-0 No 5058 *Earl of Clancarty*, 1960
When visiting the West Country in the days of steam, the problem was always whether to concentrate on the Southern or Western Region. On this occasion the attractions of the North Cornwall line and Wadebridge with their 'T9s' and Beattie 'Well tanks' had been forsaken in favour of photography on the sea wall at Teignmouth. In this almost timeless scene at this classic location, a father and his son, unencumbered by cameras, are simply enjoying the lovely sight of the 'Castle' working an eastbound excursion. How relaxed it all looks.

Right **Ashburton: '1400' 0-4-2T No 1466, 1958**

It was a pity that the South Devon Railway was not able to preserve the Dart Valley line right through to Ashburton, which had a particularly photogenic station with an all-over roof. On this warm summer evening No 1466 has run round its train and is waiting to return to the main line at Totnes. However, thanks to the efforts of the SDR, we can still enjoy the sight of a '1400' Class tank engine running alongside the River Dart between Buckfastleigh and Totnes.

Below **Tavistock South: '1400' 0-4-2T No 1434**

Like Ashburton, Tavistock South station also had an over-all roof. Although only on the secondary line from Plymouth North Road to Launceston, the station was almost main-line in size and standard, perhaps because of its earlier broad gauge origins. No 1434 is waiting to depart with a summer evening auto-train to Plymouth.

Leaving Wadebridge: '4500' 2-6-2T No 5539, 1961
In the summer of 1961 Alison and I made a memorable trip to Devon and Cornwall, and during our stay I took a number of photographs around Wadebridge. Waiting by the line just outside the town for a local train to Bodmin General to appear, we were delighted when this herd of Friesian cows appeared right on cue to complete an unforgettable photograph. The North Cornwall line can be seen curving off to the north over a bridge to the right of the '4500'.

Right **Between Dunsland Cross and Halwill Junction: 'T9' 4-4-0 No 30715, April 1960**
During the course of our trip to the West Country (see page 50) we were keen to see the 'T9' 4-4-0s, which still handled some of the workings on the Bude branch. We photographed No 30338, as well as No 30715, which is coming through the conifer plantations with its train from Bude to Okehampton, formed of two Maunsell coaches.

Below **Wenford Bridge china clay depot: '0298' 2-4-0WT No 30587**
No visit to North Cornwall was complete without photographing the Beattie 'Well tanks'. Since most photographers seemed to concentrate on the scenic stretch of line between Boscarne Junction and the depot, I thought I would include this picture of No 30587 arriving at the yard.

Between Monsal Dale and Millers Dale: '8F' 2-8-0 No 48390 and '4MT' 2-6-4T No 42291

What a tragedy that this spectacular line had to close, but I did manage to take a few photographs on it before the end. Here the heavy northbound train, of mainly power station coal, is being banked from Rowsley by the 2-6-4T seen in the second picture.

Between Upwey and Bincombe: Standard '4MT' 4-6-0 and Standard '5MT' 4-6-0, Easter Monday 1966
The visibility on this Spring day was superb, providing perfect conditions for this picture of the two locomotives climbing the 1 in 50 gradient with a train from Weymouth to Waterloo. The Isle of Portland can be seen to the right on the horizon. It is still possible to photograph trains from this position close to the old Upwey Wishing Well Halt, closed in 1957, but unfortunately the growth of vegetation on the embankment has spoiled the clear open aspect of the viewpoint.

Left **Kingston-upon-Thames: Standard '4MT' 2-6-4T No 80145, 5 February 1967**

Steam passenger trains very rarely crossed the bridge over the Thames at Kingston, but an opportunity presented itself when the Locomotive Club of Great Britain ran its 'South West Suburban' railtour. On this sunny morning No 80145 is working the section of the tour from Wimbledon Park to Shepperton.

Right **Newport, Isle of Wight: 'O2' 0-4-4T No W26 *Whitwell***

The route of the line here now forms part of the road system in Newport, but in happier days the 'O2' is pulling away from the station with a train for Ryde. I think the swans make this picture, but I also love the mellow brick of the bridge and the waterside buildings.

Between Llanbrynmair and Talerddig: Standard '4MT' 2-6-4T No 80132
While I took the black and white version, Alison took this colour picture of No 80132 making an all-out effort on the 1 in 56 gradient at milepost 62, near the summit of the climb to Talerddig, with a train from Machynlleth. The red van, on the parallel A470 road, is interesting in itself and perhaps the driver was enjoying the stirring sight of the locomotive as he overtook it.

Left **Cholsey & Moulsford: 'Modified Hall' 4-6-0 No 7921 *Edstone Hall*, August 1963**
On a fine summer evening the 'Hall' is coming through the nicely kept station with a train for Paddington. The train is mainly composed of maroon-painted Mk I stock, but the leading coach is in the Western Region's distinctive brown and cream livery.

Right **Near Edington Burtle: '2251' 0-6-0 No 3216, April 1965**
The exhaust from No 3216 is nicely reflected in the lineside dyke as the locomotive takes its train towards Glastonbury through scenery typical of the western end of Highbridge branch.

Norton, Cheshire: '9F' 2-10-0, 27 December 1965
In this very atmospheric picture, the weak winter sun has made little impression during the day on the hard frost that still coats the ground. As dusk approaches, heralding another freezing night, the '9F' hurries through the station towards Sutton Tunnel with a train of tankers. Norton station closed in 1952.

Left **Lostock Hall station and shed (24C)**
Locomotive shed interiors or yards were wonderful places for photography. In contrast there seem to be comparatively few pictures of the sheds in their setting. This view, taken on a warm summer evening, shows the wooden station buildings, the shed and yard and the huge coaling tower. Lostock Hall remained open to the end of steam on British Railways and I am sure the staff there had their patience tested to cope with the large numbers of enthusiasts who wanted to visit the depot in those last hectic days.

Right **Edge Hill shed: '5MT' 4-6-0
No 45156 *Ayrshire Yeomanry***
Of the 842 Stanier Class '5s' built, only four carried names, so there was little chance of coming across one of this quartet to photograph when the whole class was at work. No 45156 survived to the end of steam on British Railways and was used on one of the railtours that marked this event. Even though it has lost its cast nameplates, it shows signs of being cared for by the staff at Edge Hill shed where I took this photograph. It proudly carries the Edge Hill '8A' shed code on the smokebox door and 'Edge Hill (Liverpool)' on the bufferbeam. I photographed *Ayrshire Yeomanry* again at Rose Grove shed on 2 August 1968, where it had been rostered for the last steam-powered local freight working to Clitheroe.

Ashington: Ivatt '4MT' 2-6-0, 14 June 1965
I was very lucky to have such a wonderful sunset to record this train slowly crossing the viaduct over the River Wansbeck with a load of coal from Ashington Colliery. The appearance of this 2-6-0 was quite unusual since most trains were worked by 'J27' 0-6-0s or 'Q6' 0-8-0s.

Left **Leslie, Fife: 'J38' 0-6-0 No 65901, 1966**
The branch from Markinch to Leslie lost its passenger service in 1932, but in 1966 it was still open to serve Smith, Anderson (of railway photography fame) & Co's Fettykil paper mill at Leslie. The 'J38' is crossing the viaduct outside the town with some empty hoppers bound for the main line.

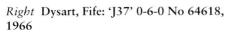

Right **Dysart, Fife: 'J37' 0-6-0 No 64618, 1966**
The lines in the Fife coalfield, centred around Thornton Junction, were very busy in the mid-1960s, not least the one south through Dysart to Kirkcaldy and Burntisland. After a passenger train has passed, the 'J37' is pulling out of the loop on its way to Burntisland. The station gardens are a superb sight and reflect the pride the station staff must have in them.

St Mary's Crossing Halt: '2800' 2-8-0 No 3866 and '5100' 2-6-2T No 4163, 15 April 1961
Happily the Gloucester to Swindon line is still open and includes a continuous climb from Standish Junction to Sapperton Tunnel with a ruling gradient of 1 in 60. In steam days this route through the picturesque Golden Valley was high on my list of locations to be visited. Assisted by the '5100' Class banker, which will probably have come on at Brimscombe, the 2-8-0 is making steady progress up the gradient with its train mainly consisting of mineral wagons.

Above **Fairford: '7400' 0-6-0PT No 7412, 30 August 1958**
A railway modeller's delight, Fairford station was surrounded by fields and located some distance to the east of the town. Paddington via Reading is 89 miles away, as the milepost by the signal shows. The Pannier tank is waiting to leave the station with the early afternoon service to Oxford.

Left **Swindon Town: '5700' 0-6-0T No 3724**
I am afraid I can't remember exactly which train this was, but it is coasting in from Swindon Junction station. The lighting conditions are very pleasing as the sun has come out after a heavy shower of rain.

Above **Severn Bridge: '1600' 0-6-0PT No 1627, 1959**

What a shame the magnificent Severn Bridge, seen in the background of this photograph, was damaged by a tanker on the night of 25 October 1960. The vessel collided with one of the piers, causing severe damage to the bridge, which was never repaired. The year before, No 1627 is about to enter the station with a train from Berkeley Road to Lydney Town.

Right **Near Whitecliff Quarry: '5700' 0-6-0PT No 3609, 1958**

The railway network in the Forest of Dean was fascinating and in 1958 I was lucky enough to make a brake-van trip through Coleford to Whitecliff Quarry, where I took a number of pictures. Rather than returning on the train, I decided to walk up the line to photograph No 3609 shortly after it left the quarry with four loaded hoppers.

Above **Near Bilston: 'King' 4-6-0 No 6005** *King George II*
From a photographic point of view the industrial nature of the Western Region main line between Birmingham Snow Hill and Wolverhampton Low Level seemed less attractive than the rather more rural sections either side of it. What is probably post-war housing forms the background to this picture of the 'King' en route to Birmingham with a train for Paddington.

Below **Wolverhampton: 'Modified Hall' 4-6-0 No 6987** *Shervington Hall*
Part of Wolverhampton racecourse forms the setting for this picture of the Birkenhead portion of a train for Paddington arriving from the Shrewsbury direction. On the other side of the viaduct are Wolverhampton Oxley sidings.

Above **Llandudno Junction: '5MT' 4-6-0s, No 44838 leading**
This very heavy summer holiday train from the North Wales coast has the benefit of two Class '5s' as its pulls out of the station bound for Chester. The train locomotive is fitted with a self-weighing tender. On the left of the picture a '4F' 0-6-0 is backing through the station on the line from Betwys-y-coed.

Right **Near Chester: '5MT' 4-6-0**
No 45231
With the city's skyline in the background, Chester's Roodee racecourse forms the setting for this photograph of No 45231 crossing the River Dee before turning off at Saltney Junction on its way to Shrewsbury.

Left **Ledbury: 'Castle' 4-6-0 No 4078 *Pembroke Castle***
This train for Worcester and Paddington has just left the station, where the double-track line from Hereford becomes single before it enters the 1,316-yard-long Ledbury Tunnel. Despite the steep sides of the embankment, which could make this location rather gloomy, there is a nice reflection off the well-cleaned locomotive.

Below **Gloucester: 'Jubilee' 4-6-0 No 45627 *Sierra Leone***
The distinctive outline of Gloucester Cathedral can be seen on the skyline at the extreme left of this picture of the 'Jubilee' approaching Tramway Junction with an express for Birmingham and through to Newcastle. This busy location was very rewarding, offering the chance to photograph both Western and London Midland trains. The Western Region shed yard is on the right.

Right **Longhope: '4300' 2-6-0 No 7335, 7 April 1961**
These 2-6-0s were regularly used on the scenic 30-mile line from Gloucester to Hereford. In lovely evening light, No 7335 is waiting to leave the station with a train for Ross-on-Wye and Hereford.

Below **Torpantau: '2251' 0-6-0 No 2218, 7 April 1961**
The name 'Torpantau' had a ring and mystique about it, one of those locations many photographers wanted to visit. Situated near the summit of the line, which reached 1,313 feet at Torpantau Tunnel, the isolated station looks at its most bleak in heavy rain as No 2218 coasts in with a train from Newport to Brecon, a 47-mile journey that will take more than 2½ hours. In the opposite direction there was a 7-mile climb from Talyllyn with a ruling gradient of 1 in 38.

Above **Manorbier: 'Manor' 2-6-0 No 7814 *Fringford Manor*, 1963**
Few railway photographers seemed to venture to the far west of Wales, but in the summer of 1963 Alison and I visited this area once again using the faithful Lambretta. It is just before half past one in the afternoon and the 'Manor', proudly displaying the 'Pembroke Coast Express' headboard, has just arrived at the resort with the through coaches to Carmarthen and Paddington. They are due to reach the capital at about a quarter to eight in the evening.

Below **Johnston: 'Hall' 4-6-0 No 4983 *Albert Hall***
In the evening the most important train from Neyland was the up 'Postal', conveying a 'Royal Mail' Travelling Post Office. The train also picked up sleeping cars at Carmarthen for Paddington, where it was scheduled to arrive at 4.40am the next morning.

Right **Near Fishguard: 'Hall' 4-6-0 No 5905 *Knowsley Hall***
I am told that No 5905 was one of the most difficult 'Halls' to see, since it spent most of its life shedded in the far west of Wales. Bearing that elusive smokebox shedplate '87J' (Goodwick), the locomotive is climbing the 1 in 50 gradient out of Fishguard with a fitted freight, containing several meat containers.

Below **Letterston Junction: '5700' 0-6-0PT**
This local train from Clarbeston Road to Fishguard has just joined the single-line section. On the back are some empty cattle wagons en route to Fishguard Harbour.

Llanbedr & Pensarn: '2251' 0-6-0 No 3213
There were many excellent photographic locations on the Cambrian Coast line from Machynlleth to Pwllheli, especially where it ran near the sea. Often the weather could be very different along the coast from what it might be a few miles inland, and this picture shows this perfectly, since by the look of the clouds over the mountains, the coast seems to be enjoying the best of the weather on this fine evening. The Collett 0-6-0 is coasting into the station with a northbound pick-up freight containing two gunpowder vans bound for Penrhyndeudraeth.

Above **Near Borth: 'Manor' 4-6-0 No 7828 *Odney Manor***
It has been a fine summer day and the sun is beginning to set. The 'Manor' and its train catch the light while climbing away from the seaside resort with a service to Aberystwyth.

Below **Tregaron: '4300' 2-6-0 No 6347**
With cotton grass flowering in the foreground, No 6347 heads towards Aberystwyth with a surprisingly long freight from Carmarthen. I think Tregaron Bog is now a national nature reserve, and in the 1960s the area was the only place in the British Isles where red kites could be seen.

Llyn Tegid (Bala Lake): '4300' 2-6-0 No 7300

What a lovely location this was, and no wonder the Bala Lake Railway chose this section for its trains after the line was closed by British Railways. On this summer day, the clouds are reflected in the water as the 'Mogul' passes the woods bordering the lake near Llangower Halt with a train from Barmouth to Ruabon.

Right **Blaenau Ffestiniog Central: '5700' 0-6-0PT No 4683 and '7400' 0-6-0PT No 7440, October 1958**
A contrast in weather, and just the sort of damp and gloomy sort of day you might expect to find in Blaenau! Long before the town became a centre for tourists, No 4683 waits to leave on its lonely journey of some 25 miles over the moors to Bala.

Below **Llanwrtyd Wells: '8F' 2-8-0 No 48434**
More wet weather in Wales! The Stanier 2-8-0s were regularly used on summer Saturday holiday trains on the Central Wales line.
In heavy rain, No 48434 looks fully the master of its task as it prepares to stop at the spa town with such a service for Swansea.

Left **Birkenhead (Woodside): '4MT' 2-6-4T No 42441**
Despite its high arched roof, what a dark gloomy station this usually was, hemmed in by tall buildings. On this occasion, however, the sun is high enough to provide just the right light for me to photograph Birkenhead shed's Stanier tank pulling out with a train for Helsby.

Above **Near Frodsham: rebuilt 'Crosti' '9F' 2-10-0**
On this cold winter day the '9F' is silhouetted against the misty sky as it crosses the River Weaver with a train largely consisting of brake-vans.

Right **Daresbury: 'Jubilee' 4-6-0 No 45654 *Hood***
No 45654 has just climbed over the Manchester Ship Canal on the West Coast Main Line, but has turned off towards Chester, passing Daresbury station, closed in 1952. On this rather menial duty for a 'Jubilee', the driver will be opening up the locomotive for the climb up through Norton to Sutton Tunnel.

Left Moore troughs: 'Jubilee' 4-6-0 No 45709 *Implacable*

I love the feeling of speed and sense of purpose about this picture. As the 'Jubilee' accelerates away from Warrington towards Crewe, the heavy spray from the back of the tender shows that it has taken its fill of water from the troughs.

Below Euxton Coal Sidings: 'Princess Royal' 4-6-2 No 46209 *Princess Beatrice*, 5 August 1961

I felt that the 'Princess Royal' 'Pacifics' exuded an immense sense of power – the long boiler barrel and the small but perfectly formed chimney made a great impression on me. No 46209 is passing Euxton on the busy stretch of line south of Preston with a very heavy inter-regional train, made up as far as I can tell of 14 coaches, typical of the time.

Warrington: 'Britannia' 4-6-2 No 70022 *Tornado*, and '5MT' 4-6-0 No 45068
There were some good photographic opportunities on the West Coast Main Line as it climbed out of Warrington over the Manchester Ship Canal. One of the 'Britannias' transferred from the Western to the London Midland Region has just crossed the River Mersey on its way south and will shortly reach the canal bridge.

At the same location one sunny winter morning, the Class '5' is pulling out of the yard towards the main line.

Above **Warrington Bank Quay: '5MT' 4-6-0 No 45317**
In a busy scene at Bank Quay looking south, an old ex-LNWR 0-8-0 is shunting the yard (extreme left), next to an up coal train that has just been given the road. Standing in the station is a train for Crewe, while overshadowed by Crosfield's huge soap works the Class '5' coasts through on the relief line.

Left **Vulcan: '5MT' 4-6-0 No 45149**
This is a rather sad picture because the great Vulcan Works, which produced steam and diesel locomotives for use all over the world, including this country, has now been demolished. Part of the stone sculpture seen on the side of the works has been saved and is now displayed at the entrance to the village, where the houses originally built for the Vulcan workers have now been restored. No 45149 has come off the Liverpool to Manchester line at Earlestown and is heading south towards Warrington.

Above Springs Branch, Wigan: '5MT' 4-6-0 and '9F' 2-10-0
I was able to obtain some very evocative pictures at this location, and it was difficult to know which to choose for this book. However, here the Class '5' on the West Coast Main Line is about to pass beneath the line from Hindley to Pemberton, which allowed trains to by-pass Wigan Wallgate.

Below Hoghton: '8F' 2-8-0
When this picture was taken, Hoghton was a pleasant rural village between Bamber Bridge and Blackburn. The long eastbound climb between those two stations steepens to 1 in 101 through Hoghton, which lost its passenger service in 1960. The '8F' makes a fine sight on this long train of empty coal wagons bound for the Yorkshire coalfields.

Left **Manchester Victoria: '5MT' 4-6-0s, January 1958**
On a snowy morning two Class '5s' blow off steam as they pause between duties at the east end of the station.

Below left **Manchester Exchange: '5MT' No 45340**
No 45340 is filling the station's roof with smoke as it pulls out with a westbound excursion one summer afternoon. A Standard Class '5' can be seen in the right background.

Above **Between Preston and Euxton Junction: 'Jubilee' 4-6-0 No 45582 *Central Provinces*, 15 October 1955**
I started my National Service in the RAF in the summer of 1955 and later that year was posted to RAF Weeton near Kirkham for an engine mechanic's course. This gave me the opportunity to make various railway visits in the North West. On this occasion I was going to Manchester, and the train I had boarded at Preston was beginning to slow down for the junction at Euxton where it would turn off to take the line through Chorley and Bolton. Leaning out of one of the windows, I was able capture the spectacular sight of No 45582 thundering south, as it overtook my train with an express from Blackpool to Euston.

Above **Grayrigg: '5MT' 2-6-0 No 42976**
Since there were only 40 locomotives in this class of Stanier-designed 'Moguls', the chance to photograph one was always welcomed, especially in a scenic location like Grayrigg where they were not very often seen. No 42976, paired with a Fowler tender, is slowly plodding up the bank towards the summit of Grayrigg with a freight train for Carlisle. This locomotive was the first of the class to be withdrawn in July 1963.

Left **Near Shap: 'Jubilee' 4-6-0 No 45670 *Howard of Effingham***
Because of the dramatic setting of the climb of the bank from Tebay, comparatively few pictures seemed to be taken on the north side from Penrith. The 'Jubilee' is working hard with a southbound express near Shap station.

Tebay: '5MT' 2-6-0 and '4MT' 2-6-4T, 1958
On this fine summer evening I am on a hillside just north of Tebay, towards the end of a day's photography on Shap. One of Tebay shed's Fowler 2-6-4Ts has just buffered up to the rear of the long freight train and the two locomotives are beginning the assault on the bank. In the background, below the village, wagons can be seen parked on the line to Kirkby Stephen, ready for return to County Durham where they will be loaded with coke for Barrow-in-Furness.

Above **Garsdale: '8F' 2-8-0 No 48080, 3 August 1961**
I made several visits to the Settle & Carlisle line, when invariably the weather was wet. However, I think the rain has enhanced this picture of a southbound anhydrite train for Widnes, coasting through the station. The Midland Railway signal controls the platform that was used by trains to Hawes.

Above right **Between Garsdale and Ais Gill: '6MT' 'Clan' 4-6-2 No 72009 *Clan Stewart*, 18 June 1965**
During their last years in service the 'Clans' were often used on local services over the Settle & Carlisle line. Unfortunately the sunlight of this fine summer evening cannot disguise the loss of nameplate and very shabby external condition of Carlisle Kingmoor's No 72009 working a stopping train from Hellifield.

Right **Hawes: '4MT' 2-6-4T No 42278, 23 January 1958**
On this snowy day I made a journey by train to Hawes and back using the afternoon service from Hellifield. In 'Christmas card' conditions, the Fairburn tank is waiting to leave on the return run. Due to the kindness of the driver, I was invited to travel on the footplate back to Hellifield, the passage through Blea Moor tunnel being unforgettable. Passenger services between Hawes and Garsdale were withdrawn in March 1959.

South of Sleaford: 'B1' 4-6-0 No 61042
I have good reason to remember this picture taken in October 1961, since it won 1st Prize in an Ian Allan photographic competition judged by the late Geoffrey Freeman Allen. Gerry Siviour, Alison and I are standing on the bank of a dyke in the late afternoon sun as the 'B1' heads south with the Liverpool and Manchester to Harwich boat train.

Above **Between County School and Dereham: 'J15' 0-6-0
No 65471**
Norwich shed kept its small remaining allocation of 'J15s' in nice
condition, as can be seen from this picture of the afternoon milk
train from North Elmham. The shed's spare 'J15', No 65471, is
working the train to Norwich, and from there the milk tanks will
be taken on to Ilford.

Below **Spalding: 'WD' 2-8-0 No 90013**
Ford cars and a motorcyclist wait patiently at the level crossing as
the 'WD' rumbles into Spalding with a freight from the Boston
line.

Left **Scunthorpe & Frodingham: '5MT' 4-6-0 No 45325**
On this sunny morning in October 1965 the Class '5' is working hard through the station with a westbound freight and will shortly commence the sharp descent towards the River Trent, which it will cross on the lifting bridge near Althorpe.

Below **Cambois: 'J27' 0-6-0, 13 June 1965**
In June 1965 my brother and I decided to make a visit to North East England, where many of the freight workings around Newcastle were still worked by steam We spent some time photographing the intensive workings to and from Ashington Colliery. How quiet the road looks, since apart from the signalman's car there is barely another vehicle in sight as the 'J27' heads north towards the colliery.

Right **Annfield Plain: '9F' 2-10-0 No 92060, 15 June 1965**
'9Fs' were used on the trains of iron ore from Tyne Dock bound for the steelworks at Consett. Since the line was steeply graded, it guaranteed some good action shots, so was high on our list of places to visit. Despite poor weather, we were able to take this picture of No 92060 hard at work with a loaded train on the climb to Consett.

Below right **Alnwick: 'K1' 2-6-0 No 62011, 14 June 1965**
After taking pictures in the Ashington area, we went on to the very short line from Alnmouth to Alnwick, often worked by 'K1' 2-6-0s. No 62011 from 52D (Tweedmouth) shed will hardly be taxed by the lightweight train for Alnmouth as it leaves the impressive and ornate station built for the Duke of Northumberland. I had last seen this locomotive on more prestigious duties on the West Highland line in 1961 (see page 99). Passenger services were withdrawn from Alnwick in January 1968.

Above **Near Beattock: 'WD' 2-10-0 No 90772**
Compared to the huge number of War Department 2-8-0s, there were only 25 of the 2-10-0 variety, so I was very pleased to secure this nice shot of No 90772 coasting down the bank with a train of tankers bound for Carlisle.

Left **Whitrope Tunnel: 'B1' 4-6-0 No 61081, 1 August 1961**
During the course of our holiday to Scotland in July 1961, which I mentioned in the introduction to this section, my brother and I took some pictures on the 'Waverley Route'. This southbound train is emerging from the tunnel past the Whitrope distant signal. Unfortunately there was a disaster with the Voightlander Bessa II camera I was using on this holiday. While we were taking photographs on the Windermere Lakeside branch on our way north, one of the shutter blades split, rendering the camera unusable. Luckily I had just enough savings in my Post Office account to enable me to buy a Zeiss Ikon Nettar camera in Glasgow as a temporary replacement, and used it for the rest of the holiday.

Right **Between Stow and Galashiels: 'V2'
2-6-2 No 60957, 31 July 1961**
The day before the picture at Whitrope, we
had come through Edinburgh and taken a
few pictures in the Galashiels area, such as
this one of the 'V2' heading south with a
train for Carlisle.

Below **Edinburgh, Princes Street Gardens: 'A4' 4-6-2 No 60011**
Empire of India **and 'A2' 4-6-2 No 60535** ***Hornet's Beauty*, July
1959**
For this holiday (see page 24) I travelled to Edinburgh from King's
Cross on the 'Elizabethan' hauled by 'A4' No 60028 *Walter K.*

Whigham. Before continuing north I took some pictures from the
footbridges over the railway in Princes Street Gardens, which
offered good vantage points to photograph the trains on this busy
stretch of line.

Above **Burntisland: 'J38' 0-6-0 No 65909, 1966**
My final railway holiday in Scotland before the end of steam was in 1966, when I took a number of pictures of the heavy goods traffic centred around Thornton Junction. The British Aluminium factory at Burntisland was served by trains of Presflo bulk alumina wagons, which are seen in this train approaching the station, where some quite large vessels can be seen moored in the adjacent docks.

Below **Benderloch: '2P' 0-4-4T No 52204, 26 July 1961**
During our 1961 summer holiday we visited the Ballachulish branch where we were lucky enough to have some good weather for a change. The old Caledonian Railway tank makes a nice picture leaving the station for Connel Ferry.

Right **Glen Lochy: '5MT' 4-6-0
No 45400, 25 July 1961**
On a typically wet Highland day, the Class
'5' has paused at this lonely crossing loop
between Tyndrum Lower and Dalmally to
await an eastbound freight train hauled by
another Class '5', No 45359, and will
shortly recommence its journey towards
Oban.

Below **Achanalt: '5MT' 4-6-0 No 45478, July 1959**
Since my first railway holiday to Scotland in July 1959 was by
train, the opportunities for photography were somewhat limited.
However, I did manage to take a few pictures on the Kyle of

Lochalsh line, and here is the Achanalt signalman taking the
single-line token from the fireman of this train bound for
Inverness.

Glenfinnan Viaduct: 'K1/1' 2-6-0 No 61997 *MacCailin Mor*, July 1959
I think this was the best picture I obtained in Scotland during my July 1959 trip. In untypical sunny weather, the 'K1/1' comes across the famous concrete viaduct with a train for Mallaig. How good it is that steam trains can still be photographed on this line today.

Above **Glenfinnan, July 1959**
After I had taken the last picture, I turned round and photographed the train going away towards the station. Bringing up the rear, and passing that so elegant distant signal, is the rebuilt 'Coronation' observation car used on the line. You can see the attendant sitting by the window at the back of the car, where he will be providing a commentary as the train makes its way towards Mallaig. I travelled in this coach on another day and was able to tape some extracts from his commentary on the small portable West German 'Phonotrix' recorder that I carried with me. I still have the 'Phonotrix' and the tapes I made with it.

Right **Near Glenfinnan: 'K1' 2-6-0 No 62011, 27 July 1961**
The weather was very wet for the journey my brother and I made along the Mallaig line – the pages of my Summer 1961 Scottish Region timetable still show signs of the soaking we received! In those days the Mallaig road, which can be seen behind the train, was not properly surfaced with tarmacadam west of Glenfinnan, so the Land Rover, which is following the train eastwards through the bleak landscape, would have been an ideal form of transport. In contrast we felt very exposed to the challenging Scottish weather on the Lambretta.

The locomotive shed

Locomotive sheds have a special significance for me since on 8 September 1950 Feltham was the location for my first shed visit and first railway photograph, taken with my parents' Box Brownie camera. I am sure many other photographers started with such modest equipment. The subject of this picture was 'S15' 4-6-0 No 30506 standing outside the shed in the drizzle – happily it was saved from scrapping and is now based on the Mid-Hants Railway. I remember that the permit issued by the Southern Region for this visit stipulated that travel to the shed had to be made by train (a little difficult for Feltham since the shed was situated a considerable distance from the station) and that your National Identity card had to be produced. I can't recall now whether the shed foreman insisted on seeing this document!

I subsequently made innumerable shed visits, often in the early days with the aid of that fabled guide *The British Locomotive Shed Directory* by Aiden L. Fuller. As well as giving directions and walking times to the sheds, the book contained itineraries for visiting all the sheds in large cities such as London, Liverpool and Manchester, and a typed supplement, detailing sub-sheds. It is a reminder of those safer times in the 1950s and 1960s, that we didn't worry about venturing into what would now be thought of as quite dangerous 'inner city' areas. I still have all my well-thumbed books listing in pencil the lines of locomotives that could be seen – what evocative documents of the age of steam these old notebooks are, especially when they record the numbers of some almost forgotten classes.

I shall never forget coming round a corner at New Cross Gate shed on the bright sunny day of 9 January 1951 to be suddenly confronted by lines of exotic(to my eyes) stored and withdrawn locomotives. Among them were 'B4X' 4-4-0s, 'I1X' 4-4-2Ts, 'E' 4-4-0s and 'O1' 0-6-0s, and, most exciting of all, two of Bulleid's partly completed 'Leader' Class, Nos 36002 and 36003.

And what wonderful names many sheds had – a roll-call of memories: 'Monument Lane', 'Brunswick', 'Heaton Mersey', 'Tebay', 'Carlisle (Kingmoor)', 'Millhouses', 'Low Moor', 'Plaistow', 'New England', 'Annesley', 'Starbeck', 'Hull (Dairycoates)', 'Kittybrewster', 'Corkerhill and Polmadie (Glasgow)', 'Nine Elms', 'Bricklayers Arms', 'Exmouth Junction', 'Old Oak Common', 'Laira (Plymouth)', 'Croes Newydd' and so on – we all have our favourites. The organised list of shed codes created by British Railways remained largely unchanged over the 20 years of the working steam era. The oval shedplates fitted at the bottom of the smokebox on nearly all locomotives were a constant source of fascination, enabling the observer to immediately identify which depot a locomotive was from. How rare it was to see a Scottish '60' series shedplate in London, though Gerry Siviour has reminded me that the odd locomotive from North of the Border might sometimes be found at Bow Works in East London when other works were too busy. What a coup for the 'spotters' of the day.

Later on, when I started railway photography in earnest, I realised what wonderful places locomotive sheds were,

'H' 0-4-4T No 31164 waits its next turn of duty at Tonbridge shed.

whether roundhouses, semi-roundhouses, through sheds, dead-end sheds, multi-road sheds, one-or-two-road sheds, end-of-branch-line sheds and so on. Each type of shed offered something for the railway photographer, which I think is shown in the pictures I have chosen for this section. I was particularly fond of the comparatively rare semi-roundhouse, as I remark in the caption for the picture of Horsham shed (75D) on page 111. While the long shed could provide some fine lighting conditions when locomotives were standing inside close to the entrance, such as on this page and page 104, the roundhouse probably offered the greatest scope for photography, even deep inside round the central turntable. In the picture of the LMR roundhouse at Gloucester on page 110, the sun shafting in through the roof has given an almost theatrical lighting effect.

While the interiors provided a rich source of material, the yards could be equally fascinating, where photographs could be had of locomotives on the turntable, taking coal and water, or being serviced. Nowadays no one would put up with the hard and filthy conditions found in locomotive sheds, so I feel lucky to have been able to record something of this aspect of the steam era. It was sad to see the progressive closure of sheds, particularly at the end of steam on the Southern Region in 1967, when forlorn groups of locomotives were hauled off to Salisbury to await their last journeys to South Wales for scrapping, which I hadn't the heart to photograph. But at least for another year or so it was still possible to capture on film the magic of the steam shed at the handful of operational depots in North West England, notably Rose Grove (24B) and Lostock Hall (24C), which played a prominent role in the last rites of BR steam working in August 1968 – thanks for those memories!

Thornton Junction shed (62A): 'B1' 4-6-0 and 'WD' 2-8-0
Locomotive sheds were wonderful places to find interesting lighting conditions. The favourably angled sunlight has dramatically transformed the dark smoky interior of this Fife coalfield shed and picked out highlights on the sides of the grimy locomotives.

Feltham shed (70B): 'M7' 0-4-4T No 30043
Bournemouth shed (71B): 'West Country' 4-6-2 No 34004
Yeovil

For some years Feltham had a small allocation of 'M7s', one of which is dwarfed by the shed's huge coaling tower. On the left of the picture, a '700' Class 0-6-0 and 'S15' 4-6-0 wait their turn to take on coal.

In contrast, the facilities at Bournemouth were quite primitive, as shown by the containers of coal being lifted by crane to fill the tender of No 34004. Possibly because the shed was located in a residential area, the provision of an intrusive coaling tower might not have been acceptable.

Brecon shed (89B): '2251' 0-6-0 No 2247 and '2MT' 2-6-0 No 46401

Heaton Mersey shed (9F): '8F' 2-8-0
Whether the shed was large or small, servicing locomotives was a filthy job. At Brecon one of the shed's staff is shovelling ash out of the pit in front of the Ivatt 2-6-0, while at Heaton Mersey the old gas lamp, picturesque as it is, only seems to emphasise the dreadful conditions that most enginemen had to endure.

Above **Hither Green shed (73C): 'C' 0-6-0 No 31498**
If you wanted to photograph lines of locomotives, Sunday was the time to visit sheds that predominantly handled freight work. Hither Green was such a shed (and it still exists) serving South East London, where no fewer than seven of its allocation of 'C' Class 0-6-0s can be seen awaiting their next turns of duty.

Left **Feltham shed (70B): '4MT' 2-6-0 No 76006 and '4MT' 2-6-4T**
Since it was fairly close to my home, I often used to visit Feltham shed in the 1950s and early 1960s. Like Hither Green it supplied locomotives for freight workings, so most of its allocation was not used at the weekend. On this Sunday afternoon the acrid smoke drifting out of its chimney shows that the 2-6-0 has just been lit up in preparation for its weekday duties.

Nine Elms shed (70A): 'Battle of Britain' 4-6-2 No 34077 *603 Squadron* I just had to include this picture of sunlight and shadow. The locomotive is standing near the entrance to the shed so the outside light has illuminated the wheels, footplating and nameplate very nicely. I don't think colour film would have coped very well with the contrasts in tone in this picture, which was much better taken in black and white.

Warrington Dallam shed (8B)
Camden shed (1B): rebuilt 'Patriot' 4-6-0 No 45528 *R.E.M.E.* and rebuilt 'Scot' 4-6-0 No 46126 *Royal Army Service Corps*

Here are two very different sheds on the London Midland Region. A good selection of the locomotives Warrington mostly supplied for local freight workings is on display in this picture, including Standard '9F' 2-10-0s, Stanier '8F' 2-8-0s and some Class '03' diesel yard shunters. By contrast Camden was a main-line passenger shed full of impressive '7P' and '8P' motive power. I think the nicely cleaned Crewe North 'Patriot', which was named in October 1959, looks most handsome, exuding a sense of capability. It is interesting to compare it with the very similar rebuilt 'Scot' behind.

Worcester shed (85A)

There is so much of interest to look at in this photograph that I thought it deserved a full page. On the left-hand side of the picture is the old Oxford, Worcester & Wolverhampton Railway works and, above that, Worcester Shrub Hill station.

Worcester shed (85A): 'Modified Hall' 4-6-0 No 7903 *Foremark Hall*
Folkestone Junction shed, sub-shed to Dover (74C): 'Battle of Britain' 4-6-2 No 34066 *Spitfire* and '5700' 0-6-0PT No 4616

These two-road sheds were of very different character. Old Oak Common's purposeful-looking 'Modified Hall' is waiting for its next turn of duty, probably a train to Paddington.

At Folkestone Junction the 'Battle of Britain' 'Pacific' provides a striking contrast to the Pannier tank, a type drafted in to replace the old 'R1' 0-6-0Ts for banking duties on the steeply graded harbour line.

Old Oak Common shed (81A): 'Castle' 4-6-0 No 5060 *Earl of Berkeley*

Old Oak Common shed, with its roundhouse buildings, offered many opportunities for striking photographs – pictures taken outside in the yard were invariably dull by comparison. Here the light flooding into the shed has been softened by the grimy windows in the wall to give a perfect level of illumination on the side of the 'Castle'.

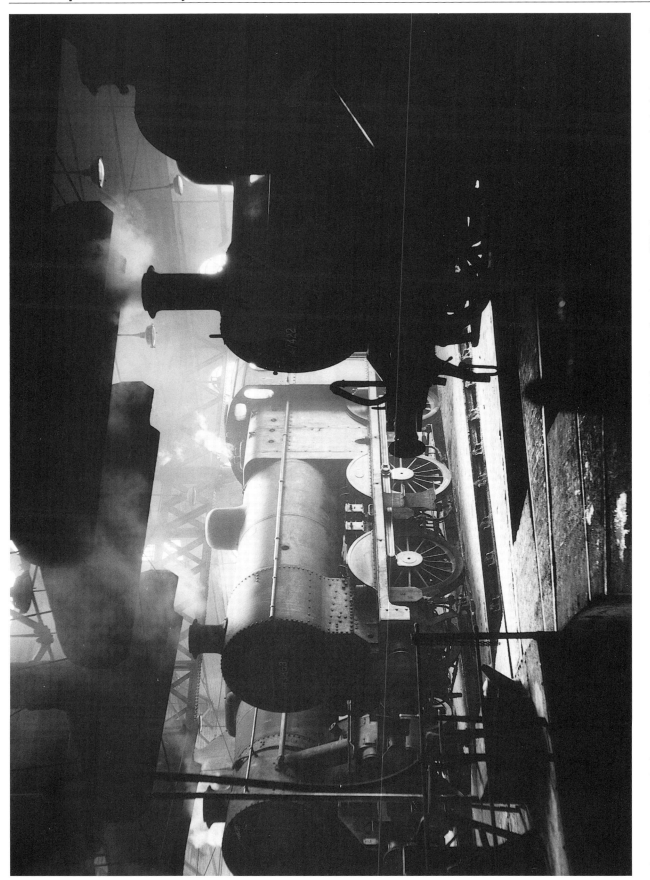

Gloucester (LMR) shed (22B)
Generally the central turntable area of a roundhouse shed was rather gloomy, making it difficult to secure good pictures. However, in this picture it almost looks as if a spotlight is shining on he '4F' in this group of locomotives crowded round the turntable. This sort of scene is very difficult to recreate convincingly in preservation, especially since only the passage of time can accumulate the coating of soot, dirt and oily grime evident in this picture.

Above **Horsham shed (75D): 'E4' 0-6-2T No 32564**
An air of unhurried calm put Horsham high on my list of favourite sheds. It was a semi-open roundhouse facing near enough west, so was well illuminated for much of the day. Occasional locomotive movements, mainly for services on the branches to Guildford or Brighton, sometimes interrupted the sound of sparrows twittering in the roof of the shed or the whine of machinery from the adjacent sawmill. The shed's 'E4', No 32564, is slumbering away in the shed between duties.

Right **Wadebridge shed (72F): '0298' 2-4-0WT No 30585, September 1961**
Another favourite Southern Region shed was Wadebridge, largely because it was the home of the three lovely Beattie 'Well tanks'. No 30585 is sandwiched between two Pannier tanks, while at the end of the line No 30587 pokes its front out into the sunlight.

Special locomotive classes

I thought it would be appropriate to include a section in the book of locomotive classes that I remember as being rather special for various reasons. Everybody will have their own favourites, and perhaps some of yours are among my selection. Of course as time went on and the end of steam came ever closer, the range of classes diminished rapidly. Particularly during the early 1960s on the Southern Region, some classes were withdrawn in toto at the stroke of a pen, usually for accounting purposes. Happily, however, there were some exceptions, when a few survivors of a venerable class soldiered on, often as a sort of protected shed 'pet' with a charmed life. Some of these 'pets' even survived the cutter's torch, such as 'B12' No 61572 at Norwich shed.

I loved the SECR 'E' Class, the last survivors being Nos 31166 and 31315. No 31315 finished its days working stopping trains over the Redhill to Reading line, while I remember seeing a well-cleaned No 31166 at Faversham shed in October 1953. To my delight this locomotive turned up at Redhill shed one sunny evening after working in from Tonbridge and the picture I took of it appears here. It wasn't until I put this selection of pictures together that I realised how many four-coupled locomotives I had included, but this reflects my love of this type of wheel arrangement, whether on a tank or tender locomotive. Many four-coupled locomotives were in use on the Southern Region into the early 1960s, notably the 'T9' Class, which was a 'must' for this section. Others that survived long after their expected

lifespan were the much loved Adams Radial tanks (page 115) and the three Beattie 'Well tanks'. Since the trio were so much associated with the Wenford Bridge line in the West Country, I thought it more appropriate to include one in the 'Steam Around Britain' section (page 63).

Of course some of the other Regions had their special last survivors, like the LT&SR 4-4-2Ts and Midland 0-4-4Ts that I made a pilgrimage to photograph in the more obscure parts of the Midlands in 1959 (page 117). The Western Region always seemed different from the other parts of British Railways, and because of its early move into standardised classes, did not have the rich variety found on other Regions like the Southern and Eastern. However, I felt that the '4700' 2-8-0s were rather special, a numerically small class with a rather old-fashioned outline for such a big locomotive and not all that easy to find and photograph (page 116). Like the Southern Region, which returned 'T9' No 120 to service in 1963, the Western Region had earlier put *City of Truro* back into working order, so I had to include a picture of this old 4-4-0 (page 116). Sadly, steam finished quickly in some parts of the country, notably on the Eastern Region, but at least I was in time to see the fabled 'Claud' Class, and a 'Glen' 4-4-0 in Scotland (page 119).

Happily, examples of the majority of the locomotives I have included in this section have been preserved to revive memories for those of us who saw them at work, as well as giving pleasure to those not old enough to have seen these veterans going about their day to day duties.

'E' Class 4-4-0 No 31166 at Redhill shed (75B) on 2 October 1954.

Ashford shed (74A): 'D' 4-4-0 No 31737, 16 August 1955; 'C2X' 0-6-0 No 32551, 18 May 1955

Ashford shed in the 1950s could always be relied upon to produce some interesting locomotive to photograph, perhaps fresh from repair in the works located on the other side of the main running line to Folkestone. The lined BR black livery seems to suit the elegant 'D' Class No 31737, a special locomotive destined to become part of the National Collection.

Although only a humble goods locomotive, how smart ex-works No 32551 looks in plain black livery. No other class of locomotive on British Railways at this time carried the double-dome boiler that I found so visually appealing. Six of the class were originally fitted with the additional dome to take the top feed fitted by L. Billinton. Although this arrangement was eventually dispensed with, the second dome remained.

Alresford: 'M7' 0-4-4T No 30125, 29 August 1957

What a delightful scene at Alresford – Eastleigh shed's 'M7' is waiting to leave with a train for Winchester, while on the other platform another service is en route to Alton. The locomotive and stock are all of LSWR origin. Thanks to the efforts of the Mid-Hants Railway, the station looks virtually the same as this today.

Right **Between Axminster and Combpyne: '0415' 4-4-2T No 30583**
On summer Sundays in the 1950s an excursion often ran from Waterloo to Exeter Central stopping at principal stations from Yeovil Junction. Detraining at Axminster and walking up the picturesque branch towards Lyme Regis, I could enjoy several hours photographing the trains. Here is No 30583 near Hart Grove Farm with an afternoon service bound for the seaside resort.

Below **Fullerton: 'T9' 4-4-0 No 30726, 1 November 1957**
Due to late deliveries and frequent failures of the then new 'Hampshire' diesel units in the autumn of 1957, Eastleigh's 'T9s' were used to keep regular services going on the lines to Andover and Salisbury. This gave railway photographers an unexpected last chance to capture them at work. No 30726 is pulling out of Fullerton bound for Andover, with a train composed of comparatively new BR Mk I stock.

Left **Litchfield (Hants): No 3440**
City of Truro
In 1957 the 'City' was brought out of retirement and, when not in use on special workings, was rostered for use on ordinary service trains, where it brought a welcome touch of glamour. A regular duty was on the Didcot, Newbury & Southampton line, where it worked the 12.42pm Didcot to Southampton Terminus and the 4.56pm return. Bound for Southampton Terminus, No 3440 is coasting into a rather run-down-looking Litchfield station, where the Didcot-bound platform is already out of use. The line closed completely in 1960.

Below **Near Moreton Sidings: '4700' 2-8-0 No 4705**
Sadly no example of this highly regarded 2-8-0 has been preserved. The class was used with equal success on heavy freight trains or express passenger turns on summer Saturdays. Since only nine locomotives were built, photographing one was always something a little special. Here No 4705 is making steady progress towards Reading along the main, rather than the relief, line with a long mixed freight.

Above **Rolleston: '1P' 0-4-4T No 58065, 9 June 1959**
The locomotive was one of the last of this Johnson Midland Railway design still working and spent its last days employed on trains between Rolleston Junction and Southwell. Surrounded by many Midland Railway features, No 58065 has just arrived at the junction with the main line from Newark to Nottingham.

Right **Near Seaton Junction: '3P' 4-4-2T No 41975, 9 June 1959**
Another long-lived survivor working out its last days on the Seaton Junction to Uppingham branch in remote Rutland was this ex-London, Tilbury & Southend Railway locomotive. At the time a pilgrimage to the branch to see this old engine was a 'must' for the railway photographer. Despite the overcast weather No 41975 makes a pleasing picture shortly after leaving Seaton Junction station.

Southport Chapel Street: '2P' 2-4-2T No 50781, January 1958 During that month I spent a week or so with my aunt and uncle who lived in Southport. Southport shed (27C) still had a few of the last Lancashire & Yorkshire Railway 2-4-2Ts left working, so I was very keen to photograph them. They were mostly used on station pilot duties, which enabled me to obtain this picture one very cold morning as No 50781 moved some empty stock out of the station.

Above **Near Maxton: '3P' 'D34' 4-4-0 No 62484** *Glen Lyon*, **1 August 1961**

On the way back south from the Highlands during our summer 1961 holiday, my brother and I particularly wanted the chance to photograph this Hawick-based 'D34' before the class disappeared for ever, although *Glen Douglas* was to survive into preservation. The foreman at the shed advised us that it was working a freight train on the Jedburgh branch. Sure enough, on this fine summer day we caught up with the 'Glen' at Roxburgh and took this photograph near Maxton as the freight returned to St Boswells.

Below **Cambridge: '3P' 'D16/3' 4-4-0 No 62582**

I wish I had been able to take more pictures of steam on the lines in East Anglia, but dieselisation came early here so the opportunities I had were very limited. However, I did secure this nice photograph of the well-cleaned 'Claud' waiting to leave with a train for Ely and Kings Lynn. In the platform on the left is a 'B17' 4-6-0, while on the right the shed looks very busy and full of locomotives.

Special trains

My photographic priority in the steam age was to concentrate on everyday workings, especially as the introduction of more modern forms of traction speeded up. However, special trains were worth following, such as the one depicted on this page, run to mark the centenary of the direct line to Portsmouth by the opening of the section from Godalming to Havant in January 1859. Apart from taking interesting routes, much of the appeal of special trains was the use of unlikely (and sometimes unsuitable!) locomotives. The poor old Adams '0395', more usually found shunting trucks in marshalling yards at places like Feltham or Wimbledon, looks a little exhausted as it is uncoupled from the train at Guildford after the run from Victoria. Special trains also gave one the opportunity to walk over the running lines where it would not be allowed on a normal day! Do note the people on the track in front of No 30567, quite surprising even for 1959, given that Guildford was in the third-rail area. Remarkably, this special, which went on to Gosport via Havant and Fareham, ran all day behind 0-6-0 goods locomotives, the other one being '700' Class No 30350. This locomotive must have had to move fairly fast in order not to delay the frequent electric services on the Portsmouth line.

Before I acquired a good camera or could afford my own transport, I did travel on a few special trains, which although most enjoyable, could be very frustrating when the light was good and one passed what looked like a fine photographic position. A particularly memorable special ran on 6 February 1955, the Railway Correspondence & Travel Society's 'The Hampshireman'. The weather for the whole day was superb, matched by wonderful motive power. 'Brighton Atlantic' No 32421 *South Foreland* took the train from Waterloo to Guildford, where it handed over to two of the hefty 'E5X' 0-6-2Ts, Nos 32570 and 32572, for the run from Guildford to Petersfield via Horsham, Pulborough and Midhurst. Finally, as the highlight of the tour, two 'T9' 4-4-0s, Nos 30301 and 30732, took the train from Petersfield back to London via Fareham and Alton over the Meon Valley line, which, like the Pulborough to Petersfield section, had just closed to passenger traffic. How I wished I had been at the lineside with photographer E. C. Griffith, who took a memorable picture of the two 'T9s' as they climbed away from West Meon in beautiful late-afternoon light after a stop at the station.

However, there were still many special trains to photograph in the years up to the end of steam. Perhaps one of the most memorable for me was the LCGB's 'Somerset & Dorset' special, which ran on a lovely day in March 1966, although the reason for it was sad since it marked the end of the much loved S&D line (page 125). Here, then, is a small selection of special trains, which I hope you will enjoy. I have concluded with two pictures of trains on the Lewes to East Grinstead line (page 126), a section of which now forms part of the modern Bluebell Railway. Although these are not 'special trains' in the accepted sense of the term, they were special in that the line had been re-opened after official closure in May 1955. Despite final closure three years later, it rose phoenix-like to become the first standard-gauge preserved line, centred on Sheffield Park, marking the beginnings of what is now a truly remarkable nationwide railway movement.

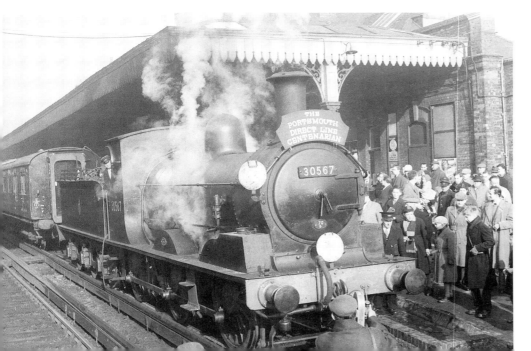

'0395' 0-6-0 No 30567 at Guildford with the special referred to above on 25 January 1959.

Right **Between Haverhill and Bartlow: 'B2' 4-6-0 No 61616** *Fallodon*, **3 May 1959**
In the 1950s members of the CURC, the Cambridge University Railway Club, enjoyed a day taking turns to operate a locomotive from Cambridge shed, under supervision. The participants could not have known that they were the pioneers for the 'Footplate Experience Courses' so popular on our private steam railways today. The 'B2' is coming through the deep cutting at Shudy Camps.

Below **Norwich City: 'B12' 4-6-0 No 61572, 8 October 1960**
Sadly, on 2 March 1959 all the Midland & Great Northern Joint lines in East Anglia closed, including the one from Melton Constable to Norwich City. To mark their passing and to help raise funds for the M&GNJ Preservation Society, this special train was run using the 'B12' that had miraculously been saved from scrapping at Norwich shed. The sight and sound of this lovely locomotive can still be enjoyed on the North Norfolk Railway, where it is based.

Above **Windsor & Eton Riverside: 'N15X' 4-6-0 No 32331 *Beattie*, 23 June 1957**
'The Riverside Special', organised by the Ramblers Association in conjunction with their Runnymede Rally, ran from London Bridge to Windsor. It was hauled by the last 'Remembrance' locomotive in service, and since this was, I think, its final duty before withdrawal, the train was a photographic 'must'. The route of the special was via Wimbledon, Weybridge, Virginia Water, the west curve at Staines, and thence to Windsor. In this picture the locomotive is waiting to leave on the return journey.

Left **Windsor & Eton Central: '9000' 4-4-0 No 9017, 20 April 1958**
Members of the Railway Enthusiasts Club from Farnborough, Hants, are full of anticipation of the day ahead, in this happy scene at the imposing ex-GWR station in Windsor. They have chartered one of the last of the 'Dukedog' 4-4-0s in service to haul 'The Severn Rambler' as far as Cheltenham. The train's principal destination was the Forest of Dean, but it also visited Sudbrook, thence to Severn Tunnel Junction. I remember that on the return journey the 'Dukedog' made a very spirited run along the main line from Severn Tunnel Junction. The locomotive is currently based on the Bluebell Railway.

Above **Merton Park: '2MT' 2-6-0 No 78038, 5 July 1964**
Now on the route of the new tram system from Wimbledon to Croydon, No 78038 is passing the junction of the line to Merton Abbey with the Locomotive Club of Great Britain (LCGB) 'Surrey Wanderer' railtour bound for Caterham. The orderly line of smartly dressed photographers have formed what is now known as a 'gallery'.

Right **Crystal Palace Low Level: 'O1' 0-6-0 No 31064, 10 November 1957**
A little dwarfed by its train of modern coaches, Stewarts Lane's nicely cleaned 'O1' is coasting into the station bound for Westerham. When I printed this negative I was delighted to see that I had also photographed that redoubtable South London enthusiast and transport bookshop owner John L. Smith (of 'Lens of Sutton' fame), seen on the extreme left wearing his trademark beret. Sadly John died in December 1999.

Above **Near Wittersham Road: 'A1X' 0-6-0Ts Nos 32662 and 32670, 11 June 1961**

The Kent & East Sussex Railway lost its passenger service in January 1954, but freight traffic lingered on from Robertsbridge to Tenterden until April 1961. To mark this final closure of the line, the LCGB's 'The South Eastern Limited' included what was left of the K&ESR in its itinerary. Unaccustomed to the sight of such a large train and the sound of No 32662 hard at work, the bullocks are panicking as the train climbs away from Hexden bridge on the way to Tenterden. Another 'Terrier', No 32670, is assisting at the rear of the train.

Below **Fort Brockhurst: 'E1' 0-6-0T No 32694 and 'O2' 0-4-4T No 30200, 30 April 1961**

It was most unusual to see an 'E1' on a passenger duty, but Fratton shed has turned out No 32694 to work in tandem with the 'O2' on this leg of the LCGB's 'The Solent Limited'. I had earlier photographed the train on the climb to Buriton hauled by 'Lord Nelson' No 30856 *Lord St Vincent*, which worked the train from Waterloo to Portsmouth Harbour. The two tank engines were in charge of the train from Fareham to Droxford, thence to Gosport and back through Fort Brockhurst to Fareham.

Right **Winsor Hill Tunnel: 'West Country' and 'Battle of Britain' 4-6-2s Nos 34006 *Bude* and 34057 *Biggin Hill*, 5 March 1966**

Another LCGB tour, another day of glorious light. The sadness that accompanied the closure of the Somerset & Dorset line was somewhat alleviated by this superb tour to mark the route's demise. The two 'Pacifics' make a wonderful sight as they climb the 1 in 50 gradient from Evercreech Junction and are about to enter the 132-yards-long, single-bore northbound tunnel.

Above East Grinstead (Low Level): 'C2X' No 32440, 28 December 1956
The facts surrounding the temporary re-opening of the Lewes to East Grinstead line, in August 1956, following its official closure in the summer of 1955, are well known, so I won't detail them here. In a picture full of atmosphere, the double-domed 'C2X' (see page 113) waits to leave for Lewes with one of the re-instated trains. Do notice the fine collection of motorbikes on the platform.

Left **East Grinstead (Low Level): '4MT' 2-6-4T No 80154, 16 March 1958**
The final British Railways trains ran between Lewes and East Grinstead on this day, although the Bluebell Railway Preservation Society would re-open part of the line in August 1960. Prior to the last down working over the line, in a scene totally different from the one above, a member of the train crew adjusts the 'bluebell' headboard on the locomotive, watched by a huge crowd of people, such was the interest in the event.

Index

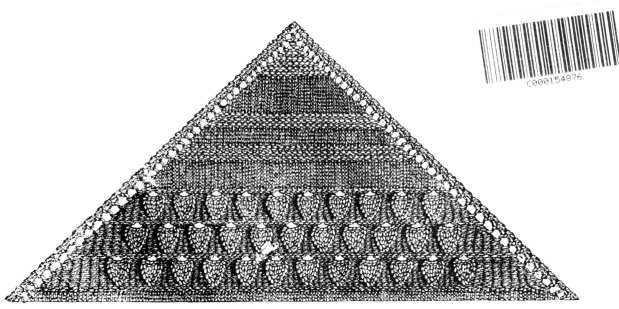

HALF OF KNITTED SQUARE FOR COUNTERPANE.

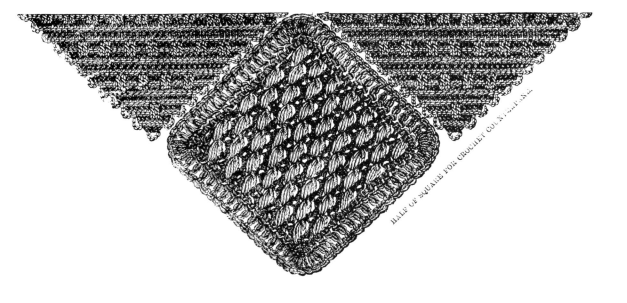

HALF OF SQUARE FOR CROCHET COUNTERPANE.

KNITTING
AND
CROCHET
·FOR THE HOME·

Shelagh Hollingworth

B. T. Batsford Ltd. London

Acknowledgements

The author would like to acknowledge the following who generously gave help, equipment and time in the preparation of this book: H. G. Twilley Ltd, Bond Knitting Systems Ltd, all the ladies who patiently made the sample articles, Judy Jordan for kindly permitting me to research the book collection belonging to her mother, Jane Koster, Jenny Edmondson for her special assistance and Brenda and Craven Elliott and Joyce and Evan Jones for their tolerant co-operation.

Photographs by Brian Hollingworth

Line drawings by Giles Hollingworth

ISBN 0 7134 5255 2

Typeset by Latimer Trend & Company Ltd, Plymouth
and printed in Great Britain by R. J. Acford Ltd, Chichester

for the publishers
B. T. Batsford Ltd
4 Fitzhardinge Street
London W1H 0AH

Contents

Introduction

The origins of knitting and crochet are acknowledged to be obscure and are wide open to speculation. For the purposes of this book we need look back no further than the Victorian era, that period of extremes of fortune in Great Britain, when the wealthy were worlds apart from the poor. Most of that social history is well documented elsewhere.

In those days the rich had very high moral standards and the time to indulge them. The ladies responded to this attitude simply by covering anything and everything with embellishment, from handkerchiefs to piano legs. On the other hand the poor, if they were in employment at all, worked such long hours that they had no spare time for handicrafts and were fortunate indeed to have even the basics of furniture, let alone fancy pieces with legs that needed covering from view.

Working-class mothers were housebound and accepted that this was their place in life. Knitting and crochet were a form of pastime that was approved for any moments of rest. They would possibly knit for the children, make gloves, socks, scarves, shawls and hats for all the family, and a variety of undergarments now long out of fashion. This would keep them busy enough, but they might also find time to work linen edgings or a bedspread for a daughter's dowry, although this would be something special, and dowry items belonged more to the upper classes.

Another group of ladies was drawn from what would now be termed the middle class – those whose wealth was too recently acquired for them to be accepted as gentry. These ladies had time on their hands but could not appear to be making items for themselves. The accepted way to make use of their spare time was to form or join knitting or sewing circles. They would meet in each others' houses, take tea and probably gossip too while they worked at their handicraft, which generally provided articles for the benefit of the poorer classes. This was indeed a strange state of affairs; the working class was literally slaving away to provide reasonably priced, ready-made items for the upper class who in turn used its spare time to produce handmade items for the poor.

Two things altered this way of life. The World Wars of this century caused attitudes to the working class to alter, primarily because women's roles in the factories changed: they had become an important labour source. The trade union movement was another prime mover in the way that factories and shops were run. People began to be better paid and this, with the influx of cheaper goods from abroad, made for better living conditions, and the necessity for handicrafts began to decline. To make things by hand could be taken by some to mean that one lacked the cash to buy ready-made. So handwork had a social stigma and knitting was confined to garments made for children. Fortunately there had been a rise in educational values and many more people were able to read and write. With this skill came the advent of printed patterns, so that although articles may not have been made in such profusion, the methods and instructions were recorded for posterity.

Knitting in particular has remained a popular pastime and in the 1960s crochet enjoyed a revival in the fashion world, but no one could have foreseen the recent, unprecedented rise in the popularity of handknit fashion wear. This is partly due to the beautiful yarns presently being manufactured and to changing attitudes to the craft. Simple and practical knitwear is still cheap enough to be purchased ready-made and with all the leisure time we have we can now knit or crochet for the pleasure it gives us.

'Back to romanticism' seems to be the keynote, and if we can take up our yarn and knitting needles or crochet hooks and make something beautiful, we can not only complement our homes with a touch of our own personality but possibly also provide an heirloom for tomorrow.

Equipment and working methods

Many of the patterns provided here are for traditional articles brought up to date. We can also take advantage of modern methods and yarns, etc. to accomplish the finest possible handwork. Reference is made to the equipment that might have been used for the original items and to suitable materials available today. It is not necessary to restrict oneself to the suggested materials – trying out different yarns with the patterns will possibly result in an entirely new and novel piece of work.

Equipment

Yarns

Most articles for the home would have been made originally in pure cotton yarns. These were cheap, readily available and pleasant to work with. They would not have the brilliant white look that today is obtained by modern technology, but white was tremendously popular in Victorian times. Indeed, this period has been described as the one of 'Victorian white knitting', referring to the articles that come under that heading, for example bedspreads (the smaller lap-rugs were also known as *couvre-pieds*), antimacassars, table linen, etc. Later, during the 1920s, experiments in the textile trades produced manmade yarns such as artificial silk (probably a term for rayon and similar threads), but these lacked one great advantage that pure cotton had: cotton could be bleached. Articles in the home needed constant washing and bleaching would have been part of that task.

In keeping, therefore, with that tradition, most of the items in this book are worked in cotton yarns. This is still the best textile to use to produce a completed article as near to the original as possible. Cotton is strong, it washes well and it will last for generations. Softer yarns might be more suitable for the baby covers, but try making these in light cotton yarns to make comfortable covers for spring or summer babies.

Knitting needles and crochet hooks

There are plenty of examples of Victorian handwork tools to be seen in museums. Not much has altered about these over the years except the materials used in their manufacture. Victorian needles and hooks were either of bone or ivory and, no doubt, occasionally they could be fashioned in wood. Between the Wars certain plastics were introduced and knitting needles became much lighter to work with. This was only partly an advantage, as the weight of the knitting was inclined to bend the needles. This made them difficult to work with and could spoil the quality of the knitting.

The Second World War produced some strange, new manmade substances, probably the most important being nylon. Nylon was thought to be the answer to everything and was used wherever possible. Not only was it spun into yarn but it could be used to form rigid items such as needles, hairbrushes, etc. These were soon displaced by the advent of other plastics with long, unpronounceable names that provided us with plastic-covered steel needles which remained rigid for the finer sizes, and solid plastic for the thicker sizes which also remained rigid. Crochet hooks were made in the same materials and a certain uniformity was arrived at. Gauges became widely available and not only were the knitting needles uniform in style, but they were also manufactured to strict size gradings that could be tested by the knitter.

Nowadays, as if to underline the saying that there is nothing new under the sun, the latest innovations in knitting needles are a return to natural materials. It is now possible to purchase knitting needles made of bamboo, wood and substances similar to whalebone. All knitting needles and crochet hooks need to be replaced periodically, especially when working in white yarns – the tips of the needles wear thin and the metal may cause the knitting to turn grey – and now might be a good time to invest in some of the latest natural-feel needles. Certainly these are the most comfortable to use with natural fibres.

Tension and measurements

This is usually the part that knitters dread most because it impresses upon them the need to keep to the tension stated on the pattern and involves making lots of little squares, when all one wishes to do is start to make the actual article. To make the items described here, the tension is not vital, although if you wish the finished piece to measure exactly the measurements given in the pattern, it will be necessary to work to the tension stated. The most important reason for considering the tension is not so much the size of the stitches as the texture of the fabric obtained by using a particular pair of needles or hook with a particular type of yarn. If the square is hard and feels solid then try again using thicker needles or hook – you are probably working too tightly. If your sample square is too floppy and perhaps has holes where there shouldn't be holes, then the square has probably been worked too loosely and a finer pair of needles or hook should be tried.

Once you have a square that is neither too hard nor too floppy, then you are ready to begin. Remember that a whole bedspread is heavy, and if it is worked too tightly it will not hang loosely over the bed. Conversely, squares worked too loosely will produce a bedspread that grows in shape before your very eyes and trails all over the floor.

The tension given in the patterns here is a guide for that particular item and indicates the needles or hook that was used to make the article in the corresponding photograph. If you want to experiment with different yarns, needles or hooks, you will come up with different tensions and measurements. This is fine provided you keep to the rule that the fabric is neither so tight that the square is solid, nor so loose that it stretches readily.

Quantities

The quantities suggested for each item are those needed to provide a finished article worked to the tension given and with the completed measurements.

The best way to check whether you are going to have sufficient yarn is first to make sure that the tension is as near to perfect as possible with your initial square, then to carry on and see how many squares you can make from one ball. The pattern will tell you how many squares are required, so simply divide the total number of required squares by the number from one ball and the result is the number of balls required for the whole article.

It is very easy to calculate the total amount you will need if you are going to design an article for yourself, as long as you build on the separate-sections principle. First, experiment with yarns and needle or hook size. Once you have produced the square you really like, draw up a chart to show exactly how you will want the pieces arranged for finishing. This is best drawn on a sheet of squared paper (see Fig. 1). Measure your original square and mark that measurement out on the paper. At this stage you will be able to add or subtract a few squares to make the finished piece as large or as small as you require it, but do remember to allow a little for seams and for borders. Now that your working chart is completed you will be able to calculate the total number of pieces, and, as described in the tension and measurements section, you will have a true guide to check the required quantities. Divide the total number of squares needed by the number of squares that can be made from one ball and you will have the number of balls required. Do not restrict yourself to the exact number – always have a little in reserve if possible. Apart from needing yarn for edgings and borders, you will need yarn for making up the article and a big item, such as a bedspread, can easily take as much as a whole extra ball.

This rule for calculating yarn requirements carries over to the borders too, especially where they are quite wide. Work a whole ball in the border pattern and note the length that is obtained. Compare this measurement with the total length required and allow a suitable amount before beginning the work.

It could be argued that if white is used then there is not the urgent necessity to set aside the total amount of yarn, but even with white there can be slight variations between dye-lots, and white shows up any difference as clearly as colour.

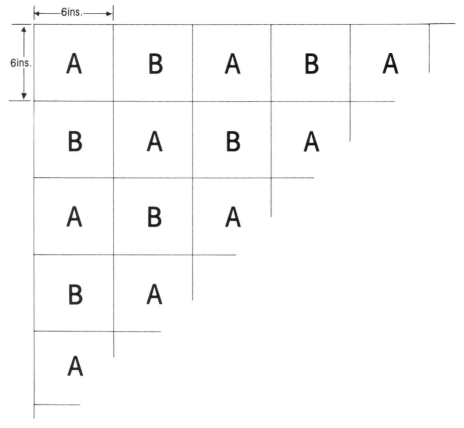

1   Draw a chart showing the position of the squares

Working methods

One of the advantages of the patterns in this book is that they are composed of small sections that are worked separately and joined together at the end of the handwork.

Since the items are meant to be worked at a leisurely pace, this piece-knitting or crochet is extremely convenient. It can be picked up and put down when there are only a few minutes to spare and it is a hobby that is easily transported. A little notebook is a useful accessory to keep a check on which row you stop at if you are suddenly called away, to note down the number of pieces as you make them and also to make sure that you are working the correct number of pieces.

Keep a close watch on the squares – it is all too easy to let some become rather loose through lack of concentration or possibly rather tight if you are working under pressure. This may not seem important but it will make the squares difficult to line up for sewing together.

Do not treat the pieces casually, for example by thrusting them down into the bottom of the knitting bag as they are finished. Keep them stored neatly and as flat as possible – this presents a much happier aspect when you come to the somewhat daunting task of making up.

As each square is finished, darn in all the loose ends. Facing the sewing together of, say, 48 or more squares is quite unnerving, but to be faced with all the ends as well could be enough to make you leave that beautiful handwork unfinished in a drawer for months. It is not a good idea to leave long ends for seaming – sew in all the ends, and if they are long enough to be used later for seaming, keep the trimmings separately for this purpose. The long ends never seem to be in the right place when it comes to making up. The correct method for joining seams is to join in new yarn as you need it, not where it happens to be at the end of making a square.

Making up

First, make certain that all the required pieces have been completed. It can be most disappointing to come to what is apparently the end of a huge piece of handwork only to find that there are some sections still to be made. Count the squares or strips, and if possible arrange them in the finished order. Simply counting the number may result in the correct number but not necessarily the order that you have visualised.

Traditional bedcovers in which the squares form an optical illusion are best sewn together with the right side of the work facing the worker (that is, with wrong sides together), using a mattress or invisible seam (see Fig. 2). This will make the join flat and virtually invisible so that, ideally, the viewer is unable to tell how the pattern has been contrived. Always join four sections into a larger square before continuing further; that is, join four small squares into a larger square until all the large squares are made, then join the large squares into lines. Finally join the lines of larger squares (see Fig. 3).

Where crochet squares are to be handsewn together these also are best joined into larger squares first. If the individual squares or strips have double crochet or trebles along the side edges these may be neatly joined with simple oversewn seams. Place the edges right sides together, work a neat oversewn seam along one side, working through the back loops of the stitches only. When turned to the right side of the work the seam is outlined by the front loops of the stitches. For joining squares, work two separate pairs of aligned squares along one edge and fasten off, then unfold the two sets of squares and place them, together, right sides facing, working

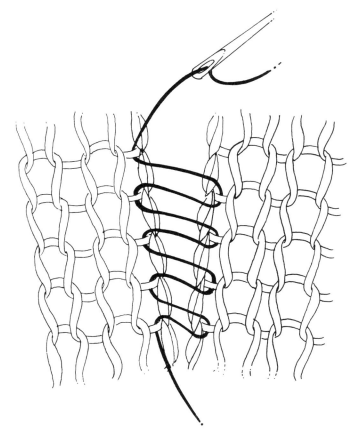

2 *Mattress seam*

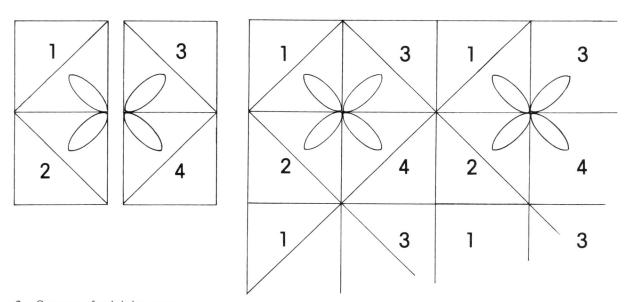

3 *Sequence for joining squares*

a seam along the adjacent sides to form a large square (see Fig. 4).

For a raised decorative effect, both knitted and crocheted sections can be joined with crochet seams. Hold two edges wrong sides together so that the edge stitches or rows may be matched exactly and, using a suitable crochet hook and matching yarn, insert the hook through both layers of fabric, draw loop through, yarn round hook and draw through loops on hook, forming a double crochet ridge on the right side of the work. It may not be appropriate to work into every stitch or row-end – adjust the double crochet to form as straight a line as possible. If the raised edge should flute or gather this will spoil the finished look.

Squares can also be joined with crochet slip stitch. Here, put the right sides of the work together and simply draw a loop through the work and through the loop on the hook before moving on to insert the hook into the next place. This method has the advantage of speed, since there is virtually no stopping to cut and re-thread the yarn as in hand sewing.

Joining the pieces into larger sections presents no difficulties but when the final seaming has to be done on a bedspread, for example, the work will be very heavy. It is best to work the last sections and the borders with the main part of the article supported upon a table.

If you have taken care to keep the individual sections relatively flat, the completed work should not require much finishing in the way of pressing, etc. Cotton yarn has a certain natural quality which ensures that the finished work stays relatively flat but does not lose its texture. Pressing should only be undertaken if it is absolutely necessary and attention must be given to the yarn label which will give full details about iron heat, etc.

Some items may be improved by 'dressing'. The article should be lightly rolled inside a dampened bathtowel and left for some hours to absorb the dampness. Then it should be carefully removed from the towel without being creased and left to dry out thoroughly in a completely flat position, ideally on an unused bed.

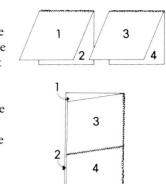

4   *Sewing order for crochet squares*

Making a start

Do not be afraid to embark on one of these projects. Remember that when you have made the first square or strip you are that much nearer to finishing. It can be very gratifying to mark off each square as you complete it.

If you would like to tackle a bedspread but feel a little daunted by the size of the task, begin by working, say, eight of the squares and joining them into a large cushion. This will provide you with a timetable from which to work and you will be able to gauge just how long a whole bedspread would take. You may carry on with the squares, and at the end you will have a matching cushion, or if you tire earlier you may unstitch the cushion cover and use the pieces to complete the bedspread.

Some of the crochet articles are joined up as they are worked. If you embark on too large a project, many of these patterns will rest quite happily as a smaller item if you wish to stop. Small squares start out as a traycloth, then they can develop into a tablecloth, and if you cannot stop they could end as a bedspread, or a full-length window screen.

For those of you in a hurry or those who do not hand knit, knitting pattern 8 is for a bedspread, to be worked on a simple chunky knitting machine system. This serves merely as a starter – machine knitters can experiment by making squares on their own machines in the wide variety of yarns that are available to them and produce either traditional-style articles in a fraction of the handknit time, or, by virtue of their individual skill, invent a whole new series of original, unique items for the home.

Most of the projects suggested in this book lend themselves to being adapted to readers' ideas. The edgings, for example, can be used on bedlinen, but worked in other yarns or colours would look equally good as shelf-edgings against natural textures such as wood, and would serve to show off your china and glass.

These patterns show how household articles have been made traditionally.There is still room for originality. Try experimenting with the patterns, using other yarns. A whole new range of exciting fabrics will appear and you will be adding a touch of your own personality to a never-ending tradition.

Basic steps in knitting and crochet

It is often assumed that knitting and crochet are crafts learned in childhood and never forgotten. However, for many these skills can be allowed to disappear completely and may only be nudged into life at the sight of some article so attractive that the viewer cannot wait to make one exactly like it.

For such readers the following elementary instructions are given, briefly covering casting on stitches, basic knit and purl, casting off, basic chain crochet, double crochet and treble. Instructions are also given for increasing and decreasing in knitting. In crochet the decreases and increases are generally given in the text since they form part of the pattern instructions.

Knitting stitches and methods

Casting on

A neat and supple cast-on edge is achieved by the two-needle method. This is worked between the stitches and is sometimes called rope edge. On no account should the following row be worked into the back of the cast-on stitches as this simply tightens the edge.

Make a slip knot and place the loop on the left-hand needle. With this needle held in the left hand, take the second needle in the right hand and insert the point of the right-hand needle into the loop from left to right. Using the right hand, take the main yarn (from the ball) under the point of the right-hand needle, round between the needles, then holding the main yarn slightly taut, draw the main yarn loop through the slip knot to form a new loop on the right-hand needle. Using the left-hand needle point transfer this new loop on to the left needle.

To make the next stitch, insert the right needle point *between* the two stitches on the left needle, wrap the main yarn round the needle point and between the needles and draw through a new loop, then transfer this loop on to the left needle as before. Repeat this movement until all the stitches are cast on.

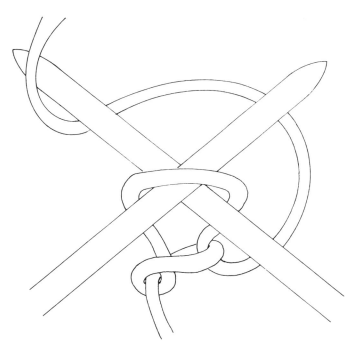

5   *Take yarn under point of needle*

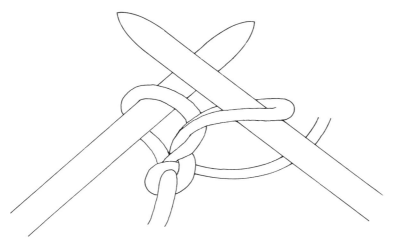

6 *Forming a new loop*

Knit stitch

Having cast on the required number of stitches, it is probably necessary to knit a tension sample and you will need to be able to work both basic knitting and purl for this purpose.

Hold the needle with the cast-on stitches in the left hand and the empty needle in the right hand. Insert the point of the right-hand needle into the first stitch on the left needle from left to right, with the main yarn at the back of the work. Now, taking the yarn in the right hand, wrap it under the point of the right needle and round between the two needle points and slightly back. With the right needle draw back the point to bring through the main yarn loop, forming a new stitch on the right-hand needle, and let the old stitch slip off the left needle point. One stitch has now been knitted. Continue in this way, knitting across the row. At the end of the row, turn the work to place the needle with the stitches in the left hand and the empty needle in the right hand.

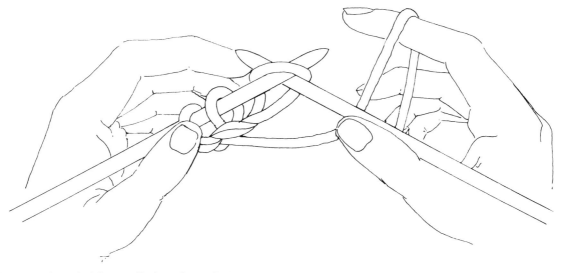

7 *Insert point of right needle into first stitch*

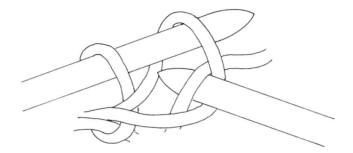

8 Draw back the point of right needle

Garter stitch is worked in this way, knitting every row. It may be made neater if the first stitch of every row is slipped knitwise (as if to knit). Where garter stitch ridges are needed in patterns it is sometimes more convenient to begin the pattern on the wrong side of the work, in which case purl rows may be specified – this will produce exactly the same effect since knit and purl simply make stitches towards either the front of the work or the back.

Purl stitch

Take the needle holding the cast-on stitches in the left hand. With the empty needle in the right hand, insert the point of the right needle into the first stitch on the left needle, from right to left, with the main yarn to the front of the work. Holding the main yarn in the right hand, take the main yarn round the point of the right needle, first between the two needle points then under the right needle, and draw the yarn back. Turning the needle right and away, draw the main yarn loop through the left loop and on to the right needle. Let the stitch slip off the left-hand needle. One stitch has been purled on to the right-hand needle. Continue in this way until all the stitches have been worked.

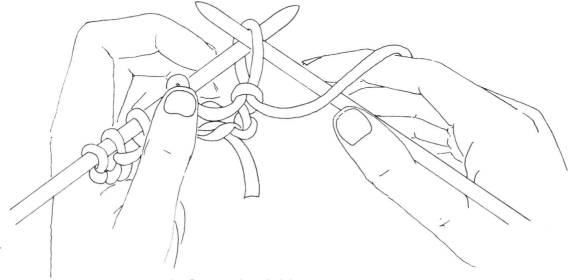

9 Insert point of right needle from right to left

18

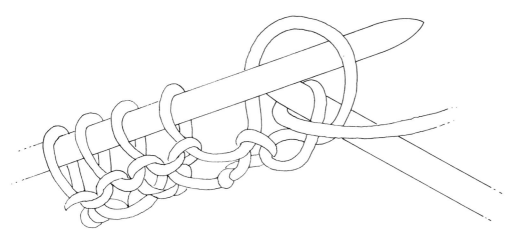

10 Draw main yarn through left loop

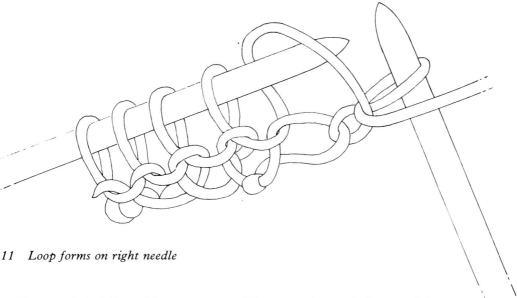

11 Loop forms on right needle

One row knit followed by one row purl forms stocking stitch, one of the most common patterns used in hand knitting. Good, even stocking stitch is essential when knitting in cotton yarns, particularly for large stretches of knitting, for example between garter-stitch ridges on bedspreads. If the stocking stitch appears to be marred by ridges, try experimenting by using a size finer needle for the purl rows – workers frequently purl more loosely than they knit.

Casting off

The directions here refer to casting off knitwise. It is sometimes more correct to cast off in pattern or rib, following the previous rows – this means knitting or purling the stitches before lifting them over and off the needle.

With the needles held as if to knit a row, work the first two stitches on to the right-hand needle. Using the point of the left needle, lift the first stitch knitted over the second stitch and off the right-hand needle. Knit the next stitch on to the right-hand needle and lift off the first stitch over the last stitch knitted. Continue in this manner along the row of stitches until just one stitch remains on the right-hand needle.

Draw out this stitch, cut the yarn to leave a long end and draw this end through the elongated stitch. Draw up tightly to secure.

Try to avoid casting off tightly unless specifically advised. Casting off has a tendency to draw in the edge anyway and a tight row could not only snap in wear but might produce problems in sewing up, since the cast-on edge is usually fairly loose and cast-off and cast-on edges are often joined together in household linens.

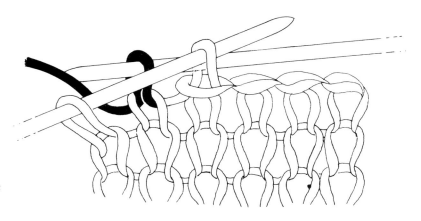

12   Work two stitches on to right needle

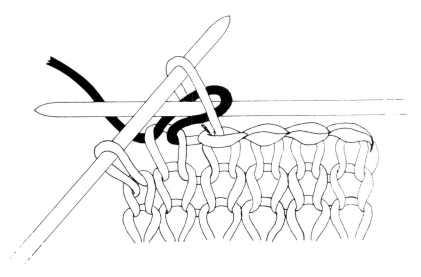

13   Lift first stitch over second stitch

Increasing

There are various methods of increasing in knitting, the most common method being simply to work twice into the following stitch. To do this, knit the next stitch in the usual way but do not let the old stitch slip off the left-hand needle. Instead, take the main yarn to the back of the work and knit into the back of the same loop and then take the old loop off the left-hand needle. Alternatively the second stitch taken from the original loop could be purled. In either case there are now two loops on the right-hand needle.

Another method of making a new stitch is to increase between stitches. Insert the point of the right-hand needle between the next two stitches, lift the loop lying between the stitches on to the left-hand needle, and knit or purl into the back of the loop. Care must be taken with this method since it does not require an actual stitch to make the increase. This particular method of increasing is always specified in the instructions, as failure to work the increase between the stitches will result in the pattern not working correctly across the row.

A decorative form of increasing is the simple 'yarn over'. This usually creates a hole on the right side of the work and is worked as follows. Take the main yarn round and over the needle before working the next stitch. On the following row, work this extra loop as a stitch. Some of the pattern instructions call for two loops to be formed before the following stitch – these will become two stitches on the next row and sometimes form a larger hole.

Decreasing

Decreases can be made at the beginning and end of rows and also in the middle. The most usual way to decrease is to work the next two stitches together. The decrease may be used to alter the actual size of the piece being worked or as decoration. Decorative decreases are specified in the pattern; for example, at one end of the motif you may be required to knit two stitches together and at the other, to knit a stitch, slip a stitch then using the point of the left-hand needle to lift the first stitch over the second. Occasionally two stitches will be decreased, either by working three stitches together by inserting the point of the right-hand needle through all three stitches on the left needle before knitting or purling, or by slipping one stitch, knitting the next two stitches together then lifting the slipped stitch over the last stitch on the right-hand needle. Stitches are also knitted or purled through the backs of the loops to produce a decorative effect.

Unless otherwise specified, when decreasing to alter the shaped pieces in the patterns, simply knit the next two stitches together.

Crochet stitches and methods

Crochet stitches are very easily formed and the same stitches may be used in a variety of ways, for all-over fabric, for decorative edgings and worked in rounds.

Making chain

Begin by making a slip knot as if for knitting. Draw this loop firmly on to the crochet hook. Hold the hook in the right hand and the yarn in the left hand. The yarn is slipped around the left hand as shown, and it will feed more comfortably into the hook if the ball of yarn is kept to the left of the worker (unlike knitting where it is more natural for the ball of yarn to be kept to the right of the worker).

Holding the hook and yarn, take the hook under the yarn (thus wrapping the yarn round the hook) and draw this loop forward and through the slip knot. One chain stitch has been made. Continue to wrap the yarn round the hook and draw loops through until the required number of chain has been made. After approximately five chain are made it is necessary to move down the chain that has been made. Hold the made chain firmly with the fingers of the left hand.

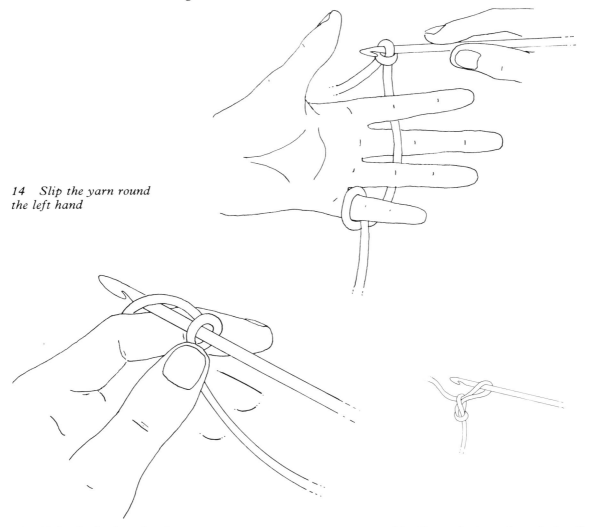

14 *Slip the yarn round the left hand*

15 *Take the hook under the yarn*

16 *Draw the loop through the slip knot*

Slip stitch

This stitch is seldom used as part of the actual pattern. It generally occurs in shaping garments and in joining rows or rounds of crochet.

Insert the hook under the *two* loops of the stitch instructed, wrap the yarn round the hook and draw the loop through.

Double crochet

Insert the hook into the next chain or the next stitch instructed, under the top *two* loops, wrap the yarn round the hook and draw the loop through, wrap the yarn round the hook again and draw through the two loops on the hook. One double crochet stitch has been made. This stitch may also be used to neaten edges by inserting the hook into the edge of the main crochet or knitting and forming double crochet stitches in the same way.

17   Draw through two loops on hook

Treble crochet

Before inserting the hook wrap the yarn round the hook, then insert the hook into the next chain or stitch instructed under the *two* top loops, wrap the yarn round the hook and draw it through the stitch (three loops on the hook). Wrap the yarn round the hook and draw through the first two loops on the hook, wrap the yarn round the hook once more and through the remaining two loops. One treble has been made. Continue in the same way across the row.

18   Three loops on the hook

Double treble

This stitch is a longer version of the treble. Wrap the yarn twice round the hook, insert the hook into the next stitch instructed, draw a loop through, yarn round hook and through the first two loops on the hook. Wrap and draw through two loops until one loop remains on the hook.

23

Half treble

This is a small version of treble that is sometimes used to form petals in Irish crochet. Wrap the yarn round the hook as if to treble, insert the hook, draw a loop through (three loops on the hook), yarn round hook and draw through all three loops together.

It is important to note that in crochet patterns it is frequently necessary to build up the depth of a row or round at its beginning, so a row may well start with a number of chain. If these chain are followed by the words 'miss one stitch' this indicates that the chain are to stand as the first stitch and should be counted and treated as a stitch on the following row or round.

Counting the rows

In both knitting and crochet the number of rows can be vital to the correct measurements. For knitting, row counters can be purchased – these slip on to the end of the knitting needle and it is a simple movement to record each row as it is worked. How can you remember to turn the counter? As each row is completed, the end of the left-hand needle slips through the left hand as the empty needle is transferred to the right hand; on every alternate row the needle with the row counter slips through in this way and the row counter touching the fingers serves as a reminder and should be turned at that very moment – note that two numbers need to be turned. This is far less trouble than marking numbers down in a notebook, although when working with four needles, or crochet, a written record of the rows is probably the safest method. Where squares are being made it is essential that exactly the same number of rows is worked for each to make the row-ends align for making up.

It is fairly easy to count rows of crochet but working in rounds usually requires the use of a marker to indicate the beginning and end of a round. Small plastic markers are now available and are recommended. These slip into the work with a twisting movement and, being plastic, they do not damage the work and are simple to remove when the article is finished.

Left-handed knitting and crochet

It is no more difficult for left-handed people to learn knitting and crochet than right-handed. The instructions should be followed but reversed by reading left for right and right for left. At the same time place a mirror by the book so that a reflection of the diagrams may be seen, showing the drawings in reverse.

Teaching the crafts

If you are teaching someone else to knit or crochet, use the instructions from the book. This is much easier for the learner than having to keep stopping to re-read the instructions. Read each part slowly and, for a right-handed learner, sit beside him or her. For the left-handed worker sit opposite to demonstrate – in this way your movements will be reflected.

Practice pieces

Tedious though it may seem, a few pieces must be made before attempting too complex an item. After learning the basic knit, purl and treble crochet, keeping a neat square and steady tension, turn to the particular pattern that you wish to make and consider whether there are any special stitches or techniques you will need in order to make that item. Just spend a little more time working a practice piece that incorporates those techniques. This will not only save time once you have embarked on a large project but could also prevent the misery of pulling out a piece of work and the possibility of a somewhat untidy area in your otherwise pristine white work.

Although some of the pattern stitches used in this book may appear complicated, all stitches are based on knit and purl, double crochet and treble crochet and any elaboration is explained in the pattern and very quickly learned. One of the great advantages of working in strips or squares is the speed, not only of working, but of learning the pattern, enabling the worker to knit or crochet without having constantly to refer to the book.

Except for the pram and cot covers, each item is worked in pure cotton. This is one of the easiest yarns to handle. It is smooth and retains its suppleness even in humid conditions, making it a perfect yarn with which to learn or refresh the memory while making these lovely old patterns.

If after looking at one of the articles in this book you feel tempted to learn or to return to knitting and crochet, be assured that after a few practice squares a novice may produce as accomplished an item as any experienced craftsman or woman. Your results will certainly be treasured in years to come.

Abbreviations

alt	alternate	ch	chain
approx	approximately	dc	double crochet
beg	begin(ning)	htr	half treble
cm	centimetre(s)	tr(s)	treble(s)
cont	continue	dtr	double treble
dec	decrease(ed)(ing)	sp	space
foll	following	yrh	yarn round hook
g	gram(s)		
in	inch(es)		
k	knit		
p	purl		
psso	pass slip stitch over		
rep	repeat		
sl st	slip stitch		
st(s)	stitch(es)		
st-st	stocking stitch		
tbl	through back of loop		
tog	together		
ybk	yarn back		
yfwd	yarn forward		
yrn	yarn round needle		

These are the abbreviations normally used in knitting and crochet patterns. Any special abbreviations are given in the text of the pattern.

Note on measurements

Only one size is given for each pattern. Where other sizes are required, calculations for measurements and quantities should be made individually (see page 9). Imperial measurements follow metric measurements in parentheses and are approximate. If you have trouble coping with metric measurements, use a modern tape measure with both types of measurements and convert the figures before working, making a note of all the measurements in your notebook.

The knitting patterns

One of the great attractions of the articles included in this section is that the result of our labour looks so intricate. There is no doubt that completing any of these patterns brings not only the satisfaction of a task well done but also the reward of praise from admirers. However, beginners need not feel that the designs are too complicated for them to work. So many of the finished pieces are made up of separate sections that after making one small part, even the novice will have practised any complex method sufficiently to carry on with the remaining patterns.

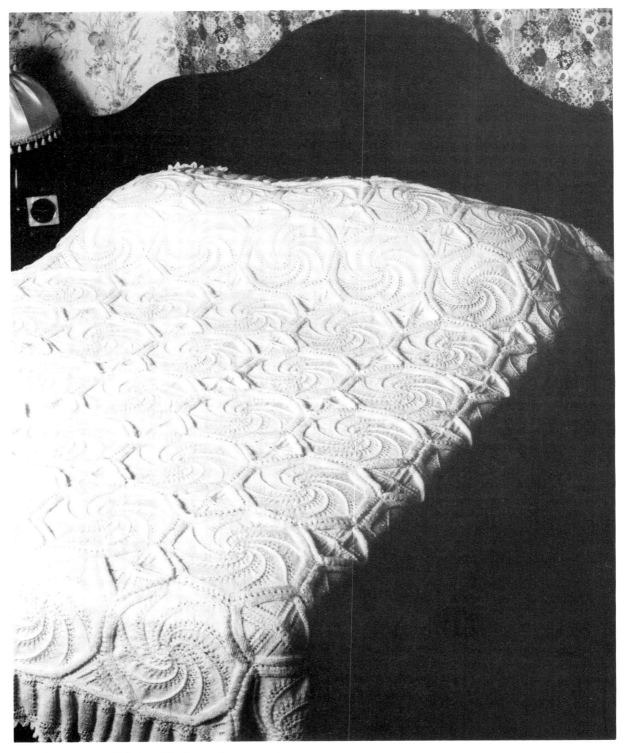

19   Octagon motif knitted bedspread, pattern 1

1 Octagon pattern bedspread

This design revives a romantic theme that is too beautiful to be hidden away for ever in old books of engravings. It has been termed 'Hungarian' but it could have come from almost anywhere. The shaped centre is octagonal and the spaces between form small squares. The sides have triangular shapes as fillers. The border is quite different in design but suits the gentle flow of the side edges and smoothly follows the rounded corners.

20   Detail of knitted octagon and square infill motif, pattern 1

Materials
36 balls (50 g) Twilley Stalite No 3 cotton
5 double-pointed $3\frac{1}{4}$ mm knitting needles

Measurements
152 cm (60 in) wide; 204 cm (80 in) long, excluding border

29

Tension

Each octagon measures 25 cm (10 in) across the centre.

Special abbreviation

M1   make 1 st by working yrn.

To make

Octagon panels   Make 48 pieces.

Cast on 8 sts (i.e. 2 sts on each of four needles and knit with the 5th needle).

Knit one round then continue in pattern thus:

1st round   *M1, k1; rep from * to end.

2nd round   K.

3rd round   *M1, k1; rep from * to end.

4th round   K.

5th round   *M1, k1, m1, k1, k2 tog; rep from * to end.

6th round   K.

7th round   *(M1, k1) 3 times, k2 tog; rep from * to end.

8th round   *K5, k2 tog; rep from * to end.

9th round   *(M1, k1) twice, m1, k2, k2 tog; rep from * to end.

10th round   *K6, k2 tog; rep from * to end.

11th round   *(M1, k1) twice, m1, k3, k2 tog; rep from * to end.

12th round   *K7, k2 tog; rep from * to end.

13th round   *(M1, k1) twice, m1, k4, k2 tog; rep from * to end.

14th round   *K8, k2 tog; rep from * to end.

Continue in this way, repeating the last 2 rounds, working 1 extra stitch before the 'k2 tog' in each repeat until the 35th round which will read:

*(M1, k1) twice, m1, k15, k2 tog; rep from * to end (*42 sts on each needle*).

36th round   *K19, k2 tog; rep from * to end.

37th and 38th rounds   P.

39th round   *P39, p twice in next st; rep from * to end.

40th and 41st rounds   P.

42nd round   *P1, (m1, p2 tog) to end along each needle.

Cast off very loosely.

Square motifs Make 35 pieces.

Cast on 8 sts (i.e. 2 sts on each of four needles and knit with the 5th needle).

1st round   *M1, k1; rep from * to end.

2nd round and every foll alt round to 18th round   K to end.

3rd round   *M1, k3, m1, k1; rep from * to end.

5th round   *M1, k5, m1, k1; rep from * to end.

7th round   *M1, k2, k2 tog, m1, k3, m1, k1; rep from * to end.

9th round   *M1, k2, k2 tog, m1, k1, m1, sl1, k1, psso, k2, m1, k1; rep from * to end.

30

11th round *M1, k2, k2 tog, m1, k3, m1, sl1, k1, psso, k2, m1, k1; rep from * to end.

13th round *M1, k2, k2 tog, m1, k5, m1, sl1, k1, psso, k2, m1, k1; rep from * to end.

15th round *M1, k2, k2 tog, m1, k7, m1, sl1, k1, psso, k2, m1, k1; rep from * to end.

17th round *M1, k2, k2 tog, m1, k9, m1, sl1, k1, psso, k2, m1, k1; rep from * to end.

19th round P to end.

20th round P to end.

21st round P to each corner and work k1, p1 in each corner st.

22nd and 23rd rounds P to end.

24th round *P1, (m1, p2 tog) to end along each needle.

Cast off very loosely.

Side triangle motifs Make 28 pieces.

With two 3¼ mm needles, cast on 1 st.

1st row M1, k1, m1.

2nd row and every foll alt row to 24th row P to end.

3rd row K1, m1, k1, m1, k1.

5th row K1, m1, k3, m1, k1.

7th row K1, m1, k5, m1, k1.

9th row K1, m1, k2, k2 tog, m1, k3, m1, k1.

11th row K1, m1, k2, k2 tog, m1, k1, m1, sl1, k1, psso, k2, m1, k1.

13th row K1, m1, k2, k2 tog, m1, k3, m1, sl1, k1, psso, k2, m1, k1.

15th row K1, m1, k2, k2 tog, m1, k5, m1, sl1, k1, psso, k2, m1, k1.

17th row K1, m1, k2, k2 tog, m1, k2, k2 tog, m1, k3, m1, sl1, k1, psso, k2, m1, k1.

19th row K1, m1, k2, k2 tog, m1, k2, k2 tog, m1, k1, m1, sl1, k1, psso, k2, m1, sl1, k1, psso, k2, m1, k1.

21st row K1, m1, k2, k2 tog, m1, k2, k2 tog, m1, k3, m1, sl1, k1, psso, k2, m1, sl1, k1, psso, k2, m1, k1.

23rd row K1, m1, k2, k2 tog, m1, k2, k2 tog, m1, k5, m1, sl1, k1, psso, k2, m1, sl1, k1, psso, k2, m1, k1.

24th and 25th rows P to end.

26th row K to end.

27th row P to end.

28th and 29th rows Rep 26th and 27th rows.

30th row P1, (m1, p2 tog) to end.

Cast off very loosely.

To make up

Back-stitch seam is most suitable for joining these motifs. With right sides of octagon motifs together sew the sections together, with six sections along the width and eight sections along the length, using just one-eighth of each side, thus leaving small square spaces between the octagons and triangle spaces at the sides. It is most convenient to join four octagons together first, then insert a square motif before moving on to the next set. When the twelve larger made-up pieces are completed join them into the finished bedspread. Finally sew in the triangle shapes to straighten the side edges.

2   Fluted border for octagon pattern bedspread

The fluted effect of this simple border is achieved by turning and working extra rows along some of the stitches. The pointed lace is knitted in with the main part of the border.

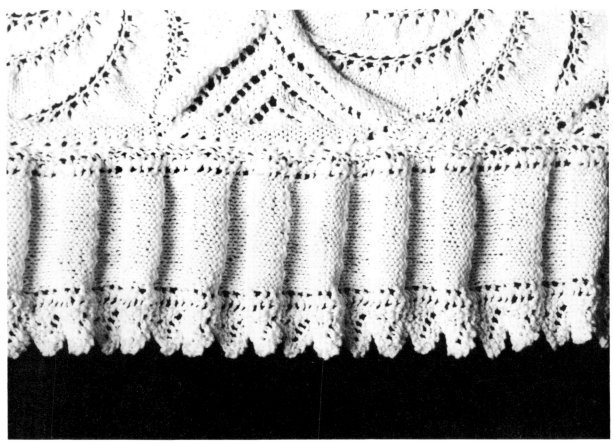

21   *Knitted fluted bedspread border, pattern 2*

Materials

11 balls (50 g) Twilley Stalite No 3 cotton
Pair $3\frac{1}{4}$ mm knitting needles

Measurements

Each strip approx 13 cm ($5\frac{1}{4}$ in) wide
Two strips to measure approx 152 cm (60 in)
Two strips to measure approx 204 cm (80 in)

To make

Cast on 25 sts very loosely.

1st row   K2, yrn, p2 tog, k16, yrn, p2 tog, k1, yfwd, k2.

2nd row   K4, yrn, p2 tog, p16, yrn, p2 tog, turn.

3rd row   Yrn, p2 tog, k16, yrn, p2 tog, k2, yfwd, k2.

4th row   K5, yrn, p2 tog, p to last 4 sts, yrn, p2 tog, p2.

5th row   K2, yrn, p2 tog, k16, yrn, p2 tog, k3, yfwd, k2.

6th row   K6, yrn, p2 tog, p to last 4 sts, yrn, p2 tog, turn.

7th row   Yrn, p2 tog, k16, yrn, p2 tog, k2 tog, (yrn) twice, k2, yfwd, k2.

8th row   K6, p1 into second of 2 made loops of previous row, k1, yrn, p2 tog, p to last 4 sts, yrn, p2 tog, k2.

9th row   K2, yrn, p2 tog, k16, yrn, p2 tog, k8.

10th row   Cast off 5 sts loosely (1 st now on right-hand needle), k2, yrn, p2 tog, k2, (yrn, k2 tog) to last 4 sts, yrn, p2 tog, turn.

11th row   Yrn, p2 tog, p16, yrn, p2 tog, k1, yfwd, k2.

12th row   K4, yrn, p2 tog, k16, yrn, p2 tog, k2.

13th row   K2, yrn, p2 tog, p16, yrn, p2 tog, k2, yfwd, k2.

14th row   K5, yrn, p2 tog, k16, yrn, p2 tog, turn.

15th row   Yrn, p2 tog, p16, yrn, p2 tog, k3, yfwd, k2.

16th row   K6, yrn, p2 tog, k16, yrn, p2 tog, k2.

17th row   K2, yrn, p2 tog, p16, yrn, p2 tog, k2 tog, (yrn) twice, k2, yfwd, k2.

18th row   K6, p1 in second made loop of previous row, k1, yrn, p2 tog, k16, yrn, p2 tog, turn.

19th row   Yrn, p2 tog, p16, yrn, p2 tog, k8.

20th row   Cast off 5 sts loosely (1 st now on right-hand needle), k2, yrn, p2 tog, p2, (yrn, p2 tog) to last 2 sts, k2.

These 20 rows form the pattern. Continue in pattern until the straight edge, when slightly stretched fits along one side edge of the bedspread. Stitches may be either cast off or left with a long end to be grafted on to the adjacent cast-on edge. For a good fit it is advisable to tack the borders on before continuing work on the remaining sections.

To make up

Join the strips to the sides of the bedspread using the mattress seam method. Either graft the cast-off stitches to the cast-on stitches, or use fine back-stitch to sew these edges together. The extra rows worked to form the fluted effect will shape the corners of the border into a natural curve.

3   Leaf pattern bedspread

The raised leaf motif in the centre of joined squares is found in many traditional bedspreads, rugs, shawls and pram or cot covers. It can bring back waves of nostalgia for long-lost household treasures, but in general it is only the leaf motif that the articles have in common; the rest of the square can have enormous variations. This may be due to the fact that the patterns were copied in the past without the method being recorded and any deviation from the original pattern would be compounded every time another knitter embarked upon a new project.

22   *Leaf pattern knitted bedspread, pattern 3*

Materials
24 hanks (100 g) Twilley Handicraft No 1 cotton
Pair 3¾ mm knitting needles

Measurements

137 cm (54 in) wide; 182 cm (72 in) long, excluding border

Tension

Each square measures 23 cm (9 in) along each side edge.

Special abbreviation and note

M1   make 1 st by working yrn.

After the first two rows, all rows begin with a slip stitch.

In the pattern, all slipped stitches should be slipped purlwise (as if to purl the stitch but slip it on to the right-hand needle).

To make

Cast on 3 sts.

1st row   (K1 and p1) both into 1st st, ybk, sl1, yfwd, (p1 and k1) both into last st.

2nd row   (K1 and p1) both into 1st st, k1, p1, k1, (p1 and k1) both into last st (*7 sts*).

3rd row   Sl1, k1, p3, k1, (p1 and k1) in last st.

4th row   Sl1, k3, m1, k1, m1, k2, (p1 and k1) in last st.

5th row   Sl1, k1, sl1, yfwd, p5, ybk, sl1, k1, (p1 and k1) in last st.

6th row   Sl1, k5, m1, k1, m1, k4, (p1 and k1) in last st.

7th row   Sl1, k1, sl1, k1, p7, k1, sl1, k1, (p1 and k1) in last st.

8th row   Sl1, k7, m1, k1, m1, k6, (p1 and k1) in last st.

9th row   Sl1, (k1, sl1) twice, p9, ybk, (sl1, k1) twice, (p1 and k1) in last st.

10th row   Sl1, k9, m1, k1, m1, k8, (p1 and k1) in last st.

11th row   Sl1, (k1, sl1) twice, k1, p11, (k1, sl1) twice, k1, (p1 and k1) in last st.

12th row   Sl1, k11, m1, k1, m1, k10, inc as before in last st.

13th row   Sl1, (k1, sl1) 3 times, p13, ybk, (sl1, k1) 3 times, inc in last st.

14th row   Sl1, k13, m1, k1, m1, k12, inc in last st.

15th row   Sl1, (k1, sl1) 3 times, k1, p15, (k1, sl1) 3 times, k1, inc in last st.

16th row   Sl1, k8, sl1, k1, psso, k11, k2 tog, k7, inc in last st.

17th row   Sl1, (k1, sl1) 4 times, p13, ybk, (sl1, k1) 4 times, inc in last st.

18th row   Sl1, k9, sl1, k1, psso, k9, k2 tog, k8, inc in last st.

19th row   (Sl1, k1) 5 times, p11, (k1, sl1) 4 times, k1, inc in last st.

20th row   Sl1, k10, sl1, k1, psso, k7, k2 tog, k9, inc in last st.

21st row   Sl1, (k1, sl1) 5 times, p9, ybk, (sl1, k1) 5 times, inc in last st.

22nd row   Sl1, k11, sl1, k1, psso, k5, k2 tog, k10, inc in last st.

23rd row   (Sl1, k1) 6 times, p7, (k1, sl1) 5 times, k1, inc in last st.

24th row   Sl1, k12, sl1, k1, psso, k3, k2 tog, k11, inc in last st.

25th row   Sl1, (k1, sl1) 6 times, p5, ybk, (sl1, k1) 6 times, inc in last st.

26th row   Sl1, k13, sl1, k1, psso, k1, k2 tog, k12, inc in last st.

27th row   (Sl1, k1) 7 times, p3, (k1, sl1) 6 times, k1, inc in last st.

28th row   Sl1, k14, sl1, k2 tog, psso, k13, inc in last st (*31 sts*).

29th to 48th rows   Continue by slipping the first st of every row and inc in last st of every row, keeping the (sl1, k1) pattern correct as previous rows.

49th row   Sl1, p to last st, inc in last st.

50th row   As 49th row.

51st row   Sl1, k to last st, inc in last st.

52nd row   As 49th row.

53rd row   As 51st row (*56 sts*).

54th row   Sl1, k1, m1, k2, k2 tog, *(sl1, k1, psso, k3, m1, k1, m1, k3, k2 tog) 4 times*, Sl1, k1, psso, k2, m1, k1, inc in last st.

55th row   As 49th row.

56th row   Sl1, k1, m1, k3, k2 tog, rep from * to * of 54th row, sl1, k1, psso, k3, m1, k1, inc in last st.

57th row   As 49th row.

58th row   Sl1, (k1, m1) twice, k3, k2 tog, rep from * to * of 54th row, sl1, k1, psso, k3, (m1, k1) twice, k1. *Do not* inc in last st.

59th row   P to end. *Do not* inc in last st.

60th row   Sl1, k2, m1, k1, m1, k3, k2 tog, rep from * to * of 54th row, sl1, k1, psso, k3, m1, k1, m1, k3.

61st row   As 59th row.

62nd row   Sl1, k3, m1, k1, m1, k3, k2 tog, rep from * to * of 54th row, sl1, k1, psso, k3, m1, k1, m1, k4.

63rd row   As 59th row.

64th row   Sl1, k4, m1, k1, m1, k3, k2 tog, rep from * to * of 54th row, sl1, k1, psso, k3, m1, k1, m1, k5.

65th and 66th rows   P to end.

67th row   K to end.

68th row   P to end.

69th row   Sl1, k65, k2 tog. This forms the first dec row.

70th row   Sl1, k2, *(m1, sl1, k1, psso, k2)* 15 times, m1, sl1, k1, psso, k2 tog.

71st row   Sl1, p to last 2 sts, p2 tog.

72nd row   Sl1, rep from * to * of 70th row 15 times, m1, sl1, k1, psso, k2 tog.

73rd row   As 71st row.

74th row   Sl1, k2, rep from * to * of 70th row 14 times, m1, sl1, k1, psso, k2 tog.

75th, 76th and 77th rows   As 71st row.

78th row   Sl1, *(k2, k2 tog, m1)* 14 times, k2 tog.

79th row   As 71st row.

80th row   Sl1, rep from * to * of 78th row 13 times, k2, k2 tog.

81st row   As 71st row.

82nd row   Sl1, rep from * to * of 78th row 13 times, k2 tog.

83rd row   As 71st row (*53 sts*).

84th row   As 71st row.

85th row   Sl1, k to last 2 sts, k2 tog.

86th row   As 71st row.

87th and 88th rows   As 85th row.

89th to 100th rows   Beginning the rows with sl1 and ending with k2 tog, work these rows keeping the continuation of the sl1, k1 pattern as in 29th to 48th rows.

101st and 102nd rows   Sl1, p to last 2 sts, p2 tog.

23   Detail of knitted leaf pattern square, pattern 3

103rd row   Sl1, k to last 2 sts, k2 tog.
104th row   As 101st row.
105th row   As 103rd row *(31 sts)*.
106th row   Sl1, k1, (ybk, sl2, k4) 4 times, ybk, sl2, k1, k2 tog. Keep yarn
at back of work loose.
107th row   Sl1, p1, (sl2, p4) 4 times, sl2, p2 tog.
108th row   Sl1, (ybk, sl2, k4) 4 times, sl2, k2 tog.
109th row   Sl1, (sl2, p4) 4 times, sl1, p2 tog.
110th row   Sl1, p to last 2 sts, p2 tog.
111th row   Sl1, k to last 2 sts, k2 tog.
112th row   Sl1, k1, (ybk, sl2, k4) 3 times, ybk, sl2, k1, k2 tog.
113th row   Sl1, p1, (sl2, p4) 3 times, sl2, p2 tog.
114th row   Sl1, ybk, (sl2, k4, ybk) 3 times, sl2, k2 tog.
115th row   Sl1, (sl2, p4) 3 times, sl1, p2 tog.
116th row   Sl1, p to last 2 sts, p2 tog.
117th row   Sl1, k to last 2 sts, k2 tog *(19 sts)*.
118th row   Sl1, k1, (ybk, sl2, k4) twice, ybk, sl2, k1, k2 tog.
119th row   Sl1, p1, (sl2, p4) twice, sl2, p2 tog.
120th row   Sl1, ybk, (sl2, k4) twice, ybk, sl2, k2 tog.
121st row   Sl1, (sl2, p4) twice, sl1, p2 tog.

122nd row　Sl1, p to last 2 sts, p2 tog.
123rd row　Sl1, k to last 2 sts, k2 tog.
124th and 125th rows　As 122nd row.
126th row　As 123rd row.
127th and 128th rows　As 122nd row.
129th and 130th rows　As 123rd row.
131st row　As 122nd row.
132nd row　As 123rd row.
133rd row　As 122nd row.
134th row　Sl1, k2 tog.
Cast off remaining 2 sts.
These 134 rows form a single square, working from one corner to the opposite diagonal corner.
Make a total of 48 squares.

To make up

These squares are best sewn together with a mattress seam, having the right side of the work facing so that each row can be joined almost invisibly. First join together four squares to form a larger square until twelve large squares have been completed. Join these large squares with three squares across the width and four squares to form the length.

4　Leaf pattern bedspread border

This is a neat border which takes up the raised leaf theme shown in the main part of the bedspread.

Materials

4 hanks (100 g) Twilley Handicraft No 1 cotton
Pair $3\frac{3}{4}$ mm knitting needles

Measurements

Each strip approx 12 cm ($4\frac{1}{2}$ in) wide
Two strips to measure approx 137 cm (54 in) each
Two strips to measure approx 182 cm (72 in) each

To make

Cast on 25 sts.
1st row　K3, k2 tog, yrn, p4, yfwd, k1, yrn, p4, yrn, p2 tog, p1, (yrn, p2 tog, k1) twice, yfwd, k2.

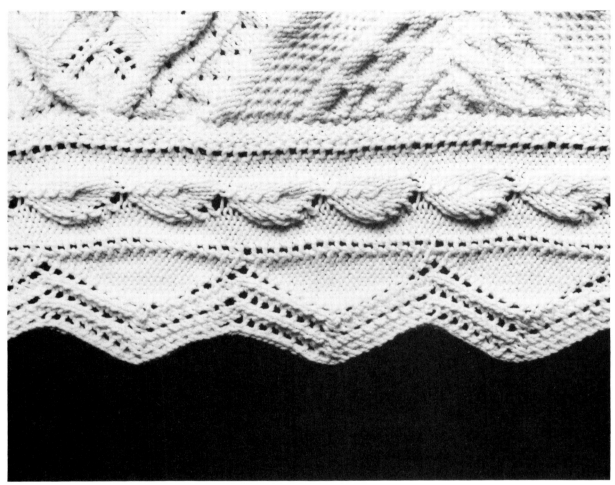

24 Knitted leaf pattern border, pattern 4

2nd row   P8, k8, p3, k9.
3rd row   K3, k2 tog, yrn, p4, yfwd, k3, yrn, p4, yrn, p2 tog, p2, (yrn, p2 tog, k1) twice, yfwd, k2.
4th row   P8, k9, p5, k9.
5th row   K3, k2 tog, yrn, p4, yfwd, k5, yrn, p4, yrn, p2 tog, p3, (yrn, p2 tog, k1) twice, yfwd, k2.
6th row   P8, k10, p7, k9.
7th row   K3, k2 tog, yrn, p4, yfwd, k7, yrn, p4, yrn, p2 tog, p4, (yrn, p2 tog, k1) twice, yfwd, k2.
8th row   P8, k11, p9, k9.
9th row   K3, k2 tog, yrn, p4, k3, sl1, k2 tog, psso, k3, p4, yrn, p2 tog, p5, (yrn, p2 tog, k1) twice, yfwd, k2.
10th row   P8, k12, p7, k9.
11th row   K3, k2 tog, yrn, p4, k2, sl1, k2 tog, psso, k2, p4, yrn, p2 tog, p6, (yrn, p2 tog, k1) twice, yfwd, k2.

12th row   P8, k13, p5, k9.

13th row   K3, k2 tog, yrn, p4, k1, sl1, k2 tog, psso, k1, p4, yrn, p2 tog, p7, (yrn, p2 tog, k1) twice, yfwd, k2.

14th row   P8, k14, p3, k9.

15th row   K3, k2 tog, yrn, p4, sl1, k2 tog, psso, p4, yrn, p2 tog, p8, (yrn, p2 tog, k1) twice, yfwd, k2.

16th row   P8, k15, p1, k9.

17th row   K3, k2 tog, yrn, p4, yfwd, k1, yrn, p4, yrn, p2 tog, p6, p2 tog, (yrn, k2 tog, k1) 3 times.

18th row   P3, k1, p2, k1, p2, k13, p3, k9.

19th row   K3, k2 tog, yrn, p4, yfwd, k3, yrn, p4, yrn, p2 tog, p5, p2 tog, (yfwd, k2 tog, k1) 3 times.

20th row   P3, k1, p2, k1, p2, k12, p5, k9.

21st row   K3, k2 tog, yrn, p4, yfwd, k5, yrn, p4, yrn, p2 tog, p4, p2 tog, (yfwd, k2 tog, k1) 3 times.

22nd row   P3, k1, p2, k1, p2, k11, p7, k9.

23rd row   K3, k2 tog, yrn, p4, yfwd, k7, yrn, p4, yrn, p2 tog, p3, p2 tog, (yfwd, k2 tog, k1) 3 times.

24th row   P3, k1, p2, k1, p2, k10, p9, k9.

25th row   K3, k2 tog, yrn, p4, k3, sl1, k2 tog, psso, k3, p4, yrn, p2 tog, p2, p2 tog, (yfwd, k2 tog, k1) 3 times.

26th row   P3, k1, p2, k1, p2, k9, p7, k9.

27th row   K3, k2 tog, yrn, p4, k2, sl1, k2 tog, psso, k2, p4, yrn, p2 tog, p1, p2 tog, (yfwd, k2 tog, k1) 3 times.

28th row   P3, k1, p2, k1, p2, k8, p5, k9.

29th row   K3, k2 tog, yrn, p4, k1, sl1, k2 tog, psso, k1, p4, yrn, p2 tog, p2 tog, (yfwd, k2 tog, k1) 3 times.

30th row   P3, k1, p2, k1, p2, k7, p3, k9.

31st row   K3, k2 tog, yrn, p4, sl1, k2 tog, psso, p4, yrn, sl1, p2 tog, psso, (yfwd, k2 tog, k1) 3 times.

32nd row   P8, k7, p1, k9 (*25 sts*).

These 32 rows form the border pattern. Repeat them until strip, when slightly stretched, measures 137 cm (54 in). Cast off loosely.

Work another strip to this length, then work two more strips, each to be approx 182 cm (72 in) when slightly stretched. Cast off at end of each strip.

To make up

Using a mattress seam, join the strips to the side edges of the bedspread, fitting the strips right to the corners, plus approx 5 cm (2 in) overlap. When all four strips are sewn, fold back the overlap to the wrong side of the work to form a mitred corner. Using a mattress seam join the mitred corners, then neatly sew down the excess fabric to the wrong side of the work.

5 Canterbury bell bedspread

Little flower-shaped bells decorate this bedspread which truly lends itself to the cottage-garden image. The square motif, which is worked from corner to corner, was recorded as long ago as 1873.

25   Knitted Canterbury bell pattern bedspread, pattern 5

Materials
31 hanks (100 g) Twilley Handicraft No 1 cotton
Pair 4 mm knitting needles
3·5mm crochet hook

Measurements
152 cm (60 in) wide; 204 cm (80 in) long, excluding fringe

Tension

Each square measures 25 cm (10 in) along each side.

Special abbreviation and note

M1 make 1 st by working yrn.
Slip all slipped stitches knitwise unless otherwise stated.

To make

With 4 mm needles, cast on 1 st.

1st row M1, k1.

2nd row M1, k1, m1, k1.

3rd row Sl1, k1, m1, k1, m1, k1.

4th row K to end.

5th row Sl1, k1, m1, k2, m1, k2.

6th row and foll alt rows to 18th row Sl1, k to end.

7th row Sl1, k1, m1, k4, m1, k2.

9th row Sl1, k1, m1, k6, m1, k2.

11th row Sl1, k1, m1, k8, m1, k2 (*14 sts*).

13th row Sl1, k1, m1, p10, m1, k2.

15th row Sl1, k1, m1, p12, m1, k2.

17th row Sl1, k1, m1, p14, m1, k2.

19th row Sl1, k1, m1, k16, m1, k2.

20th row Sl1, k1, p18, k2.

21st row Sl1, k1, m1, k18, m1, k2 (*24 sts*).

22nd row Sl1, k to end.

23rd row Sl1, k1, m1, p20, m1, k2.

24th row Sl1, k to end.

25th row Sl1, k1, m1, p22, m1, k2.

26th row Sl1, k1, p24, k2.

27th row Sl1, k1, m1, k24, m1, k2.

28th row Sl1, k1, p26, k2.

29th row Sl1, k1, m1, p26, m1, k2.

30th row Sl1, k to end.

31st row Sl1, k1, m1, p28, m1, k2.

32nd row Sl1, k to end.

33rd row Sl1, k1, m1, p30, m1, k2.

34th row Sl1, k to end (*36 sts*).

35th row Sl1, k1, m1, k2, *turn and cast on to right-hand needle 5 sts, turn, k3; rep from * 9 times more, m1, k2.

36th row Sl1, k1, p4, *k5, p3; rep from * 9 times more, k2.

37th row Sl1, k1, m1, k3, *p2 tog, p1, p2 tog, k3; rep from * 9 times more, k1, m1, k2.

38th row Sl1, k1, p5, *k3, p1, p2 tog; rep from * ending last rep, k3, p4, k2.

39th row Sl1, k1, m1, k4, *sl1 purlwise, p2 tog, psso, k2; rep from * 9 times more, k3, m1, k2.

40th row Sl1, k1, p to last 2 sts, k2 (*43 sts*).

41st row Sl1, k1, m1, k4, rep from * of 35th row 11 times, k5, m1, k2.

42nd row Sl1, k1, p6, rep from * of 36th row 11 times, p3, k2.

43rd row Sl1, k1, m1, k5, rep from * of 37th row 11 times, k3, m1, k2.

44th row Sl1, k1, p7, rep from * of 38th row, ending last rep p6, k2.

45th row Sl1, k1, m1, k6, rep from * of 39th row, ending last rep k7, m1, k2.

46th row As 40th row (*50 sts*).

47th row Sl1, k1, m1, k6, rep from * of 35th row 12 times, ending last rep k7, m1, k2.

48th row Sl1, k1, p8, rep from * of 36th row 12 times, ending last rep p7, k2.

49th row Sl1, k1, m1, k7, rep from * of 37th row 12 times, ending last rep k8, m1, k2.

50th row Sl1, k1, p9, rep from * of 38th row 12 times, ending last rep p8, k2.

51st row Sl1, k1, m1, k8, rep from * of 39th row 12 times, ending last rep k9, m1, k2.

52nd row As 40th row (*57 sts*).

53rd row Sl1, k1, m1, p to last 2 sts, m1, k2.

54th row Sl1, k to end.

55th row Sl1, k1, m1, p to last 2 sts, m1, k2.

56th row Sl1, k to end (*61 sts*).

57th row Sl1, k1, m1, p3 tog, p to last 5 sts, p3 tog, m1, k2.

58th row Sl1, k to end.

59th row Sl1, k1, m1, p3 tog, p to last 5 sts, p3 tog, m1, k2 (*57 sts*).

60th row Sl1, k1, p to last 2 sts, k2 (*57 sts*).

61st row Sl1, k1, m1, k3 tog, k7, rep from * of 35th row 12 times, k4, k3 tog, m1, k2.

62nd row Sl1, k1, p9, rep from * of 36th row, ending last rep p9, k2.

63rd row Sl1, k1, m1, k3 tog, k6, rep from * of 37th row 12 times, k3, k3 tog, m1, k2.

64th row Sl1, k1, p8, rep from * of 38th row 12 times, ending p5, k2.

65th row Sl1, k1, m1, k3 tog, k4, rep from * of 39th row, k3, k3 tog, m1, k2.

66th row As 40th row.

67th row Sl1, k1, m1, k3 tog, k5, rep from * of 35th row 11 times, k3, k3 tog, m1, k2.

68th row Sl1, k1, p8, rep from * of 36th row, p4, k2.

69th row Sl1, k1, m1, k3 tog, k4, rep from * of 37th row, k2, k3 tog, m1, k2.

70th row Sl1, k1, p7, rep from * of 38th row, p3, k2.

71st row Sl1, k1, m1, k3 tog, k2, rep from * of 39th row, k2, k3 tog, m1, k2.

72nd row Sl1, k1, p to last 2 sts, k2 (*45 sts*).

73rd row Sl1, k1, m1, k3 tog, k3, rep from * of 35th row 10 times, k2, k3 tog, m1, k2.

74th row Sl1, k1, p7, rep from * of 36th row, p2, k2.

75th row Sl1, k1, m1, k3 tog, k2, rep from * of 37th row, k1, k3 tog, m1, k2.

76th row Sl1, k1, p6, rep from * of 38th row, p1, k2.

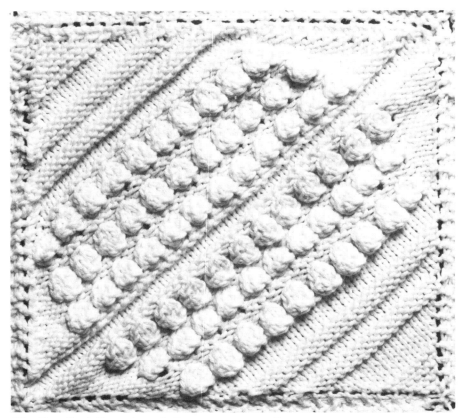

26   *Detail of Canterbury bell square, pattern 5*

77th row	Sl1, k1, m1, k3 tog, rep from * of 39th row, k1, k3 tog, m1, k2.
78th row	Sl1, k1, p to last 2 sts, k2.
79th row	Sl1, k1, m1, p3 tog, p to last 5 sts, p3 tog, m1, k2.
80th row	Sl1, k to end.
81st row	Sl1, k1, m1, p3 tog, p to last 5 sts, p3 tog, m1, k2.
82nd row	Sl1, k to end.
83rd row	Sl1, k1, m1, p3 tog, p to last 5 sts, p3 tog, m1, k2.
84th row	Sl1, k to end.
85th row	Sl1, k1, m1, k3 tog, k to last 5 sts, k3 tog, m1, k2.
86th row	Sl1, k1, p to last 2 sts, k2.
87th row	Sl1, k1, m1, k3 tog, k to last 5 sts, k3 tog, m1, k2.
88th row	Sl1, k to end.
89th row	Sl1, k1, m1, p3 tog, p to last 5 sts, p3 tog, m1, k2.
90th row	Sl1, k to end.
91st row	Sl1, k1, m1, p3 tog, p to last 5 sts, p3 tog, m1, k2.
92nd row	Sl1, k1, p to last 2 sts, k2.
93rd row	Sl1, k1, m1, k3 tog, k to last 5 sts, k3 tog, m1, k2.
94th row	Sl1, k1, p to last 2 sts, k2.
95th row	Sl1, k1, m1, p3 tog, p to last 5 sts, p3 tog, m1, k2.

96th row   Sl1, k to end.

97th to 102nd rows   Rep 95th and 96th rows.

103rd row   Sl1, k1, m1, k3 tog, k to last 5 sts, k3 tog, m1, k2.

104th row   Sl1, k to end.

105th to 108th rows   Rep 103rd and 104th rows.

109th row   (K2 tog) twice, k1, (k2 tog) twice.

110th row   K2 tog, k1, k2 tog.

111th row   Sl1, k2 tog, psso.

Fasten off.

These 111 rows form a single square, working from one corner to the opposite diagonal corner.

Make a total of 48 squares.

To make up

With right side of work facing, join four squares into a larger square, using mattress seam and aligning the rows where possible. When twelve large squares have been formed, join these in the same way with three large squares across the width and four large squares to form the length.

Cut the remaining yarn into 27 cm (11 in) lengths. With crochet hook, using four lengths together, make a tasselled fringe, hooking each tassel approximately 2.5 cm (1 in) apart. Separate each tassel into two lots of four strands and knot with its neighbouring four strands 2.5 cm (1 in) below. Separate the resulting strands into two lots of four strands and knot these below the original hooked loop (see Fig. 27). Trim the ends if necessary.

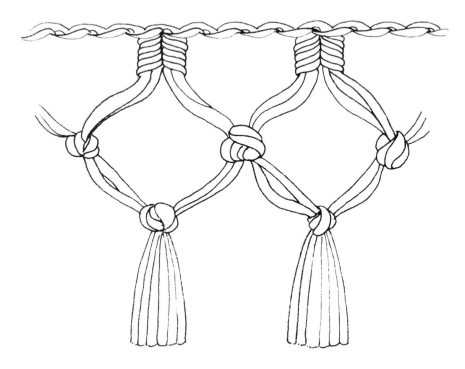

27   Making a tasselled border

6 Blackberry and smock pattern bedspread

This is a simple alternating patterned bedcover, the squares of which are worked vertically and rely on the texture of the traditional Aran patterns to provide character. Keep a close watch on the numbers of squares that you work or they may not line up for finishing as you want them to.

28 Knitted blackberry and smock squares bedspread, pattern 6

Materials
32 hanks (100 g) Twilley Handicraft No 1 cotton
Pair 4 mm knitting needles
Cable needle

Measurements

177 cm (70 in) along each side edge, excluding border

Tension

Each square measures 25 cm (10 in) along each side edge.

Blackberry pattern squares   Make 25 pieces.

Cast on 58 sts. Knit 1 row.

Continue in pattern thus:

1st row   (right side) K1, p to last st, k1.

2nd row   K1, *p3 tog, (k1, p1, k1) all in next st; rep from * to last st, k1.

3rd row   K1, p to last st, k1.

4th row   K1, *(k1, p1, k1) all in next st, p3 tog; rep from * to last st, k1.

These 4 rows form the pattern. Continue in pattern until work measures 25 cm (10 in), ending after 2nd or 4th pattern row.

Knit 1 row. Cast off.

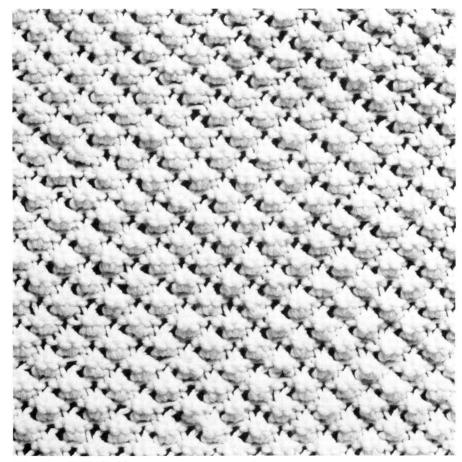

29   Detail of blackberry pattern, pattern 6

Smock pattern squares   Make 24 squares.

Cast on 76 sts.

1st row   (right side) K1, p2, *k2, p2; rep from * to last st, k1.

2nd row   K3, *p2, k2; rep from * to last st, k1.

3rd row   K1, p2, *slip next 6 sts on to cable needle, wind yarn 4 times clockwise round these sts then work (k2, p2, k2) into these sts, p2; rep from * to last st, k1.

4th row   As 2nd row.

5th and 6th rows   As 1st and 2nd rows.

7th row   K1, p2, k2, p2, *cable and wind yarn round next 6 sts as on 3rd row, p2; rep from * to last 5 sts, k2, p2, k1.

8th row   As 2nd row.

These 8 rows form the pattern. Continue in pattern until work measures 25 cm (10 in) ending after nearest 8th pattern row.

Cast off loosely.

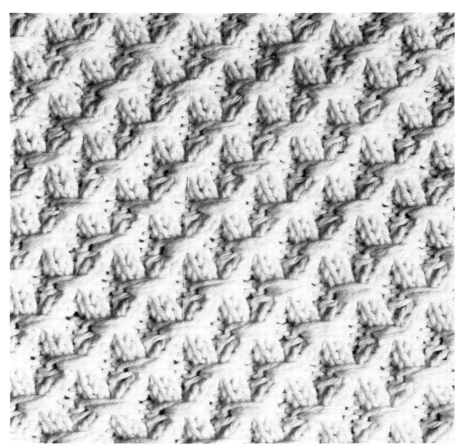

30   *Detail of smock pattern, pattern 6*

To make up

Form the squares into lines as indicated in the diagram on page 10. This

48

will present a blackberry pattern square at each corner. The edges of the squares are best joined with a back-stitch seam, since the stitch and row numbers vary. For the neatest seaming, join the squares alternately into strips, then join the strips in one seam each.

7 Garter-stitch border

The very first knitting stitch that we learn is used here to make a smooth, flexible border for the blackberry and smock pattern bedspread. The borders may be worked in one continuous strip if desired, turning the corners as given and simply continuing along the following side. On the bedcover illustrated, the borders were made in four sections and grafted together after they were fitted to and sewn on to the main part.

The slipped stitch at the beginning of every row forms a neat, firm edge – this method is advisable for any garter-stitch work.

Materials
6 hanks (100 g) Twilley Handicraft No 1 cotton
Pair 4 mm knitting needles

Measurements
11 cm ($4\frac{1}{4}$ in) wide; approx 177 cm (70 in) long

Tension
21 sts and 34 rows to 10 cm (4 in)

To make
Cast on 22 sts, very loosely.
1st row K to end.
2nd row Sl1 knitwise, k to end.
Repeat 2nd row until strip, slightly stretched, measures the same as one side of bedspread.

To turn corner curve

1st row Sl1, k to last 2 sts, with yarn at back sl next st purlwise to right-hand needle, turn.
2nd row Ybk, sl the slipped st to right-hand needle, thus wrapping the yarn around the slipped st to avoid making a hole at the turn, k to end.
3rd row Sl1, k to last 4 sts, sl and wrap the next st as on 1st row, turn.
4th row As 2nd row.

5th row Sl1, k to last 6 sts, sl and wrap the next st as on 1st row, turn.
6th row As 2nd row.

Continue in this way until the row 'sl1, k1, sl and wrap the next st, turn' has been worked. Slip the slipped stitch back on to right-hand needle and knit to end. **

Repeat from the 1st row to ** twice more.

The work may be left on a spare needle for grafting or, if preferred, may continue along the second side. Where the work is continuous around all four sides, graft the stitches after the last corner to the cast-on edge. In all cases it is advisable to tack the border to the main part of the bedspread as it is worked to ensure a good fit.

If the border is worked as four equal strips, the corners may be grafted together or, if cast off, the ends of the strips should be neatly back-stitched together.

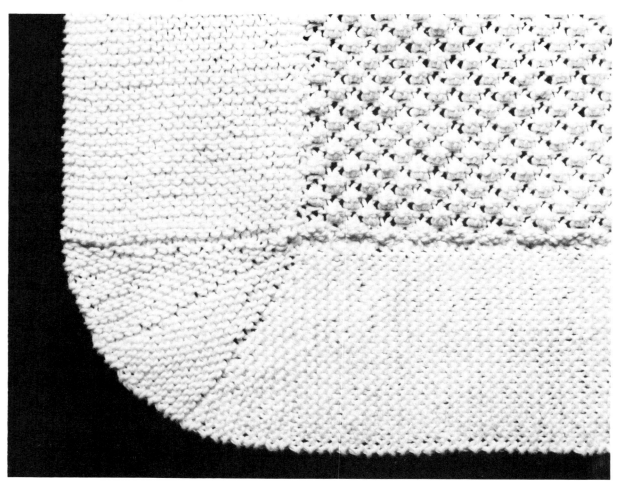

31 Garter-stitch border detail, pattern 7

8 Machine-worked bedspread

This design is also composed of small squares joined to make larger squares. The basic pattern is extremely simple, and experienced knitters could use this pattern as a basis for working more elaborate bedspreads.

The yarn used is relatively thick and a machine suitable for chunky yarns was used for the example shown here, but the principle would lend itself to almost any knitting machine. The squares are joined with double crochet to form a raised pattern for added interest and the edges are in crochet crab-stitch pattern.

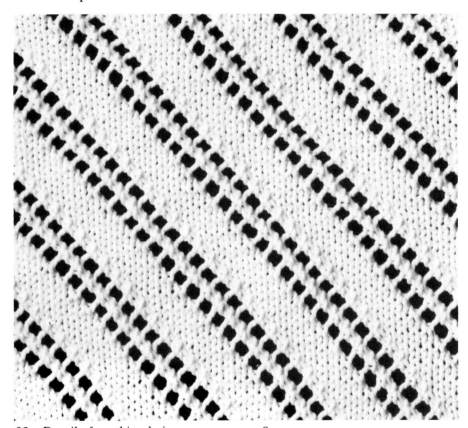

32   *Detail of machine-knit square, pattern 8*

Materials
28 hanks (100 g) Twilley Handicraft No 1 cotton
4 mm crochet hook
This bedspread was made on the **Bond knitting system**.

33   *Machine-worked bedspread, pattern 8*

Measurements
182 cm (72 in) wide; 243 cm (96 in) long

Tension
16 sts and 26 rows to 10 cm (4 in) in pattern using Keyplate 2

Square 1   Make 24 pieces.
Using closed-edge method, cast on 52 sts.
Knit 3 rows, ending carriage on right.
Continue in pattern thus:
1st row   Beg. at right-hand side, miss 4 sts, *(miss 1 st, transfer next st to missed needle at right-hand side) twice, miss 4 sts*; rep from * to * across the row, leaving empty needles in working position with latches open, k the row.
2nd row and foll alt rows   K the row.
3rd row   Miss 3 sts, rep from * to * of 1st row, leaving empty needles in working position with latches open, k the row.
5th row   Miss 2 sts, rep from * to * of 1st row across the row, leaving empty needles in working position with latches open, k the row.
Continue in this way, moving the pattern diagonally to the right until 78 pattern rows have been worked and joining new stitches into pattern as soon as possible at left-hand side.
Knit 3 rows. Cast off.

Square 2   Make 24 pieces.
Work as square 1, reversing the direction of the diagonal pattern thus:
1st row   Beg at left-hand side, miss 4 sts, *(miss 1 st, transfer next st to last missed st at left-hand side) twice, miss 4 sts*; rep from * to * across the row, leaving empty needles in working position with latches open, k the row.

To make up
With wrong sides together of one square 1 and one square 2, using crochet hook, *insert hook through both layers of fabric, draw loop through, yrh and through loops on hook; rep from * to end of side. Fasten off. Work the next two corresponding squares together in the same way. Using the same double-crochet method work the two sets of two squares together. Next join these larger squares together with double crochet, with three large squares across the width. Finally join the four strips of three squares with double crochet.

   To work the crab-stitch edging (see Fig. 34), work 1 row of double crochet all round the outer edge of the bedspread, working 3 double crochet in each corner; *do not turn*. To form the crab stitch, work 1 double crochet in each double crochet, working from left to right. Join with slip stitch to first double crochet. Fasten off.

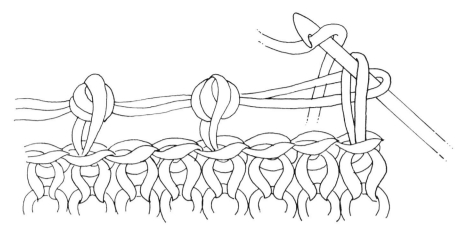

34   Crab-stitch crochet edging

9   Lace and moss stitch pattern tablecloth

This tablecloth will bring images of ladies with time on their hands, time to work beautiful articles and time to appreciate handmade linens. With the labour-saving devices available today, many of us can find time to create lovely things for the home and we can be secure in the knowledge that they will outlast many of the machine-made goods and will be popular with generations to come.

The cloth is worked in one piece, on quite a large number of stitches, but in this case when the first square is finished, the whole cloth will be finished. The lace diamond pattern is given first and is referred to throughout the pattern instructions. Once these few rows have been accomplished the knitting will become relatively simple.

Materials
17 balls (25 g) Twilley Crysette Super No 3 cotton
Pair 3¼ mm knitting needles

Measurements
Approx 91 cm (36 in.) along each side

Tension
24 sts to 10 cm (4 in) in pattern

35   *Knitted lace and moss stitch tablecloth, pattern 9*

Special abbreviations
M2   make two stitches by winding yarn twice round the needle. Note that each loop is worked separately on the following row.

Diamond pattern
1st row   *K5, k2 tog, m2, k2 tog, k4*.
2nd row   *P7, k1, p5*.
3rd row   *K3, (k2 tog, m2, k2 tog) twice, k2*.
4th row   *P5, k1, p3, k1, p3*.
5th row   *K1, (k2 tog, m2, k2 tog) 3 times*.
6th row   *(P3, k1) 3 times, p1*.
7th row   As 3rd row.
8th row   As 4th row.
9th row   As 1st row.
10th row   As 2nd row.

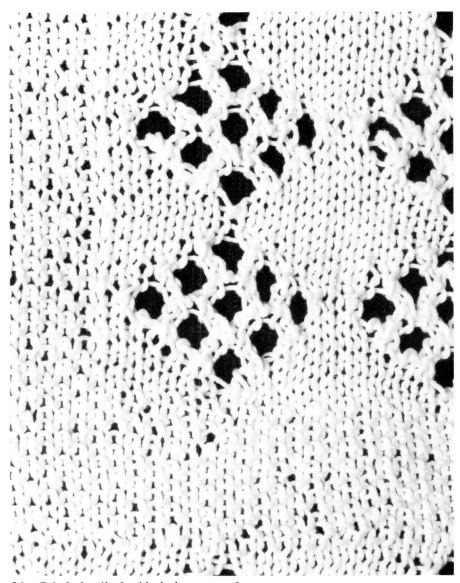

36   *Stitch detail of tablecloth, pattern 9*

To make

Cast on 220 sts.

Continue in moss stitch thus:

1st row   *K1, p1; rep from * to end.

2nd row   *P1, k1; rep from * to end.

These 2 rows form the moss stitch pattern. Repeat them until work measures 4 cm (1½ in). Now continue in diamond pattern with moss stitch borders at each end of row, placing stitches thus:

**1st row*   Moss st 12 sts, k to last 12 sts, moss st 12.

2nd row   Moss st 12 sts, p to last 12 sts, moss st 12.

3rd row   Moss st 12 sts, work from * to * of 1st diamond patt row to last 13 sts, k1, moss st 12.

4th row   Moss st 12 sts, work from * to * of 2nd diamond patt row to last 13 sts, p1, moss st 12.

Continue in this way, working subsequent diamond pattern rows until the 12th row has been completed which reads:

Moss st 12 sts, work from * to * of 10th diamond patt row to last 13 sts, p1, moss st 12.

13th and 14th rows   As 1st and 2nd rows.**

The work now continues with two outer moss stitch borders having a diamond panel between.

***15th row*   Moss st 12 sts, k14, moss st to last 26 sts, k14, moss st 12.

16th row   Moss st 12 sts, p14, moss st to last 26 sts, p14, moss st 12.

17th row   Moss st 12 sts, work from * to * of 1st diamond patt row over next 13 sts, k1, moss st to last 26 sts, work from * to * of 1st diamond patt row over next 13 sts, k1, moss st 12.

18th row   Moss st 12 sts, work from * to * of 2nd diamond patt row over next 13 sts, p1, moss st to last 26 sts, work from * to * of 2nd diamond patt row over next 13 sts, p1, moss st 12.

19th row   Moss st 12 sts, work from * to * of 3rd diamond patt row over next 13 sts, k1, moss st to last 26 sts, work from * to * of 3rd diamond patt row over next 13 sts, k1, moss st 12.

20th row   Moss st 12 sts, work from * to * of 4th diamond patt row over next 13 sts, p1, moss st to last 26 sts, work from * to * of 4th diamond patt row over next 13 sts, p1, moss st 12.

21st row   Moss st 12 sts, work from * to * of 5th diamond patt row over next 13 sts, k1, moss st to last 26 sts, work from * to * of 5th diamond patt row over next 13 sts, k1, moss st 12.

22nd row   Moss st 12 sts, work from * to * of 6th diamond patt row over next 13 sts, p1, moss st to last 26 sts, work from * to * of 6th diamond patt row over next 13 sts, p1, moss st 12.

23rd row   As 19th row.

24th row   As 20th row.

25th row   As 17th row.

26th row   As 18th row.

27th row   As 15th row.

28th row   As 16th row.***

The work will now have diamond patterns across the centre and between the moss stitch borders. Continue thus:

1st row   Moss st 12 sts, k14, moss st 12, k144, moss st 12, k14, moss st 12.

2nd row   Moss st 12 sts, p14, moss st 12, p144, moss st 12, p14, moss st 12.

3rd row   Moss st 12, work from * to * of 1st diamond patt row across next 13 sts, k1, moss st 12, work from * to * of 1st diamond patt row across centre 143 sts, k1, moss st 12, work from * to * across next 13 sts, k1, moss st 12.

4th row   Moss st 12, work from * to * of 2nd diamond patt row across next 13 sts, p1, moss st 12, work from * to * of 2nd diamond patt row across centre 143 sts, p1, moss st 12, work from * to * of 2nd diamond patt row across next 13 sts, p1, moss st 12.

5th row Moss st 12, work from * to * of 3rd diamond patt row across next 13 sts, k1, moss st 12, work from * to * of 3rd diamond patt row across centre 143 sts, k1, moss st 12, work from * to * of diamond patt row across next 13 sts, k1, moss st 12.

6th row Moss st 12, work from * to * of 4th diamond patt row across next 13 sts, p1, moss st 12, work from * to * of 4th diamond patt row across centre 143 sts, p1, moss st 12, work from * to * of 4th diamond patt row across next 13 sts, p1, moss st 12.

7th row Moss st 12, work from * to * of 5th diamond patt row across next 13 sts, k1, moss st 12, work from * to * of 5th diamond patt row across centre 143 sts, k1, moss st 12, work from * to * of 5th diamond patt row across next 13 sts, k1, moss st 12.

8th row Moss st 12, work from * to * of 6th diamond patt row across next 13 sts, p1, moss st 12, work from * to * of 6th diamond patt row across centre 143 sts, p1, moss st 12, work from * to * of 6th diamond patt row across next 13 sts, p1, moss st 12.

9th row Moss st 12, work from * to * of 7th diamond patt row across next 13 sts, k1, moss st 12, work from * to * of 7th diamond patt row across centre 143 sts, k1, moss st 12, work from * to * of 7th diamond patt row across next 13 sts, k1, moss st 12.

10th row Moss st 12, work from * to * of 8th diamond patt row across next 13 sts, p1, moss st 12, work from * to * across centre 143 sts, p1, moss st 12, work from * to * of 8th diamond patt row across next 13 sts, p1, moss st 12.

11th row Moss st 12, work from * to * of 9th diamond patt row across next 13 sts, k1, moss st 12, work from * to * of 9th diamond patt row across centre 143 sts, k1, moss st 12, work from * to * of 9th diamond patt row across next 13 sts, k1, moss st 12.

12th row Moss st 12, work from * to * of 10th diamond patt row across next 13 sts, p1, moss st 12, work from * to * of 10th diamond patt row across centre 143 sts, p1, moss st 12, work from * to * of 10th diamond patt row across next 13 sts, p1, moss st 12.

13th and 14th rows Rep 1st and 2nd of these last rows. Repeat the last 14 rows until work measures approx 76 cm (30 in), ending after nearest 14th row.

Now repeat from *** to ***, then repeat from ** to **.

Work in moss stitch for 4 cm (1½ in) to match beginning of cloth.

Cast off firmly.

To complete

Darn in ends neatly along side edges.

Should the work require pressing, pass the iron only lightly over the work to avoid flattening the texture of the pattern. Dressing the fabric (see page 13) is particularly suitable for this item.

10   Lace swirl table linen

This set of large centre mat, place mats and coasters is worked mainly in stocking stitch. The swirl effect is achieved by turning and knitting extra rows over a calculated number of stitches. The same principle is followed over all the pieces and the pointelle lace-edged borders are worked in with the main sections.

Materials
8 balls (25 g) Twilley Lyscordet No 5 cotton
This quantity will make a centre mat, four place mats and four coasters; for separate items:
Centre mat, 2 balls Twilley Lyscordet
Four place mats, 3 balls Twilley Lyscordet
Four coasters, 3 balls Twilley Lyscordet
Pair 3 mm knitting needles

Measurements
Large mat, 38 cm (15 in) in diameter
Place mats, 23 cm (9 in) in diameter
Coasters, 15 cm (6 in) in diameter

Tension
30 sts and 38 rows to 10 cm (4 in) measured over stocking stitch

To make
The centre mat
Cast on 45 sts, loosely, and slip all slipped sts purlwise.
1st row   Sl1, k39, yrn, p2 tog, k1, yfwd, k2.
2nd row   K4, yrn, p2 tog, p38, turn, leaving 2 sts.
3rd row   Sl1, k37, yrn, p2 tog, k2, yfwd, k2.
4th row   K5, yrn, p2 tog, p36, turn, leaving 4 sts.
5th row   Sl1, k35, yrn, p2 tog, k3, yfwd, k2.
6th row   K6, yrn, p2 tog, p34, turn, leaving 6 sts.
7th row   Sl1, k33, yrn, p2 tog, k2 tog, (yrn) twice, k2, yfwd, k2.
8th row   K6 p1 into second of two made loops on 7th row, k1, yrn, p2 tog, p32, turn, leaving 8 sts.
9th row   Sl1, k31, yrn, p2 tog, k8.
10th row   Cast off 5 sts loosely (1 st now on right-hand needle), k2, yrn, p2 tog, p30, turn, leaving 10 sts.
11th row   Sl1, k29, yrn, p2 tog, k1, yfwd, k2.
12th row   K4, yrn, p2 tog, p28, turn.
13th row   Sl1, k27, yrn, p2 tog, k2, yfwd, k2.
14th row   K5, yrn, p2 tog, p26, turn.

37   *Circular lace swirl knitted table linen, pattern 10*

15th row   Sl1, k25, yrn, p2 tog, k3, yfwd, k2.

16th row   K6, yrn, p2 tog, p24, turn.

17th row   Sl1, k23, yrn, p2 tog, k2 tog, (yrn) twice, k2, yfwd, k2.

18th row   K6, p1 into second made loop of previous row, k1, yrn, p2 tog, p22, turn.

19th row   Sl1, k21, yrn, p2 tog, k8.

20th row   Cast off 5 sts loosely (1 st now on right-hand needle), k2, yrn, p2 tog, p20, turn.

Continue in this way, working 2 sts less before turning on wrong-side rows until the 39th row has been worked.

40th row   Cast off 5 sts loosely (1 st now on right-hand needle), k2, yrn, p2 tog, p2, (yrn, p2 tog) to last 2 sts, p2.

These 40 rows form one pattern repeat. Work 7 more repeats of the 40-row pattern to form a complete circle. The stitches may be cast off and seamed to the cast-on edge but grafting is recommended for the join, so as to imply continuous knitting.

To complete

If the seam is to be grafted, do not cast off the stitches but leave with a long end. If the stitches have been cast off, use mattress seam with the right side of the work facing to sew the cast-off and cast-on edges together, aligning the stitches as closely as possible.

The place mats

Cast on 25 sts loosely and slip all slipped sts purlwise.

1st row   Sl1, k19, yrn, p2 tog, k1, yfwd, k2.

2nd row   K4, yrn, p2 tog, p18, turn, leaving 2 sts.

3rd row   Sl1, k17, yrn, p2 tog, k2, yfwd, k2.

4th row   K5, yrn, p2 tog, p16, turn, leaving 4 sts.

5th row   Sl1, k15, yrn, p2 tog, k3, yfwd, k2.

6th row   K6, yrn, p2 tog, p14, turn, leaving 6 sts.

7th row   Sl1, k13, yrn, p2 tog, k2 tog, (yrn) twice, k2, yfwd, k2.

8th row   K6, p1 into second loop of two made loops on 7th row, k1, yrn, p2 tog, p12, turn.

9th row   Sl1, k11, yrn, p2 tog, k8.

10th row   Cast off 5 sts loosely (1 st now on right-hand needle), k2, yrn, p2 tog, p10, turn.

11th row   Sl1, k9, yrn, p2 tog, k1, yfwd, k2.

12th row   K4, yrn, p2 tog, p8, turn.

13th row   Sl1, k7, yrn, p2 tog, k2, fwd, k2.

14th row   K5, yrn, p2 tog, p6, turn.

15th row   Sl1, k5, yrn, p2 tog, k3, yfwd, k2.

16th row   K6, yrn, p2 tog, p4, turn.

17th row   Sl1, k3, yrn, p2 tog, k2 tog, (yrn) twice, k2, yfwd, k2.

18th row   K6, p1 into second loop of two made loops of previous row, k1, yrn, p2 tog, p2, turn.

19th row   Sl1, k1, yrn, p2 tog, k8.

20th row   Cast off 5 sts loosely (1 st now on right-hand needle), k2, yrn, p2 tog, p2, (yrn, p2 tog) 8 times, p2.

These 20 rows form one pattern repeat. Work 11 more repeats of the 20-row pattern to form a complete circle.

To complete

Cast off stitches or leave to graft and complete as instructed for the centre mat.

38 Knitted place mat of table linen, pattern 10

The coasters

Cast on 15 sts loosely and slip all slipped sts purlwise.

1st row Sl1, k9, yrn, p2 tog, k1, yfwd, k2.
2nd row K4, yrn, p2 tog, p8, turn, leaving 2 sts.
3rd row Sl1, k7, yrn, p2 tog, k2, yfwd, k2.
4th row K5, yrn, p2 tog, p6, turn, leaving 6 sts.
5th row Sl1, k5, yrn, p2 tog, k3, yfwd, k2.
6th row K6, yrn, p2 tog, p4, leaving 6 sts.
7th row Sl1, k3, yrn, p2 tog, k2 tog, (yrn) twice, k2, yfwd, k2.

8th row   K6, p1 in second loop of two made loops of previous row, k1, yrn, p2 tog, p2, turn, leaving 8 sts.

9th row   Sl1, k1, yrn, p2 tog, k8.

10th row   Cast off 5 sts loosely (1 st now on right-hand needle), k2, yrn, p2 tog, (yrn, p2 tog) 3 times, p2.

These 10 rows form one pattern repeat. Work 15 more repeats of the 10-row pattern to form a complete circle.

To complete

Cast off stitches or leave to graft and complete as instructed for the centre mat.

11   Pleated teacosy

39   *Pleat-knitted teacosy, pattern 11*

Most of us are familiar with this garter-stitch cosy. Sometimes it is worked in alternate colours but this example is worked in thick white cotton throughout. Cotton serves as splendid insulation and the cosy will wash and wear well.

A pompon completes the top but a crochet or knitted loop at the top will serve as a hanger when the cosy is not in use.

Materials
2 hanks (100 g) Twilley Handicraft No 1 cotton
Pair 4 mm knitting needles

Tension
The stocking-stitch tension is 20 sts and 24 rows to 10 cm (4 in). If you obtain that tension in stocking stitch your tension will be correct for this pattern.

Note
Wind each hank into a ball and label one ball A and one ball B.
Make two pieces.
With ball A, cast on 98 sts.
Work 6 rows garter stitch (every row knit).
Continue in garter stitch as follows, working the pleats by carrying yarn not in use tightly across the back of the work.
1st row K 1A, (8B, 8A) to last st, 1B.
2nd row Twisting yarns at beg of row to avoid leaving holes, K 1B, (8A, 8B) to last st, 1A.
Repeat last 2 rows until work measures 17 cm (6½ in) ending after a wrong-side row.

Shape top
1st row K 1A, (with B, k2 tog, k4, k2 tog, with A, k2 tog, k4, k2 tog) to last st, k 1B.
2nd row K 1B, (6A, 6B) to last st, 1A.
3rd row K 1A, (with B, k2 tog, k2, k2 tog, with A, k2 tog, k2, k2 tog) to last st, 1B.
4th row K 1B, (4A, 4B) to last st, 1A.
5th row K 1A, (with B, k2 tog twice, with A, k2 tog twice) to last st 1B.
6th row K 1B, (2A, 2B) to last st, 1A.
7th row K 1A, (k2 tog B, k2 tog A) to last st, 1B.
Thread remaining stitches on to 2 strands of yarn and pull up to tighten.
Fasten off securely, leaving a long end.

To make up
Join the side seams leaving approx 10 cm (4 in) free for the teapot handle and spout, each opening to be approx 4 cm (1½ in) from cast-on edge.

Use remaining yarn to form a pompon and sew the pompon to the top to conceal the join.

If preferred a small loop may be made thus: cast on 20 sts. Cast off the sts. Fasten off. Join the two ends to form a circle and sew to the top of the cosy.

12   Bedlinen edgings

40   Knitted edging for bedlinen, pattern 12

Just a very little time and expense can transform your bedlinen into something to treasure. Adding handwork to bedlinen is no longer an old-fashioned thing to do – the standards of our forebears are now appreciated again and all types of crafts are treated with great respect.

One pattern decorates the linen in the photograph, and two alternatives are suggested. There are many more patterns for this type of edging and most of them use a few stitches and rows, making it a simple task and one that can be conveniently carried around so that a few more rows may be added when a moment arises.

Materials
2 balls (25 g) Twilley Lyscordet No 5 cotton to make sheet edging (see measurements)
2 balls to make one pillowslip edging
Pair 2¾ mm knitting needles

Measurements
8 cm (3 in) wide; sheet edging 182 cm (72 in) long; each pillowslip 102 cm (40 in) long

Tension
Knitting needles should be used with this yarn to produce strips with a width of 8 cm (3 in).

To make
Cast on 17 sts.
Foundation row Sl1, k2, yfwd, (k2 tog) twice, k2, k2 tog, yfwd, k3, yfwd, k1, yfwd, k2. This row is not repeated.
1st row Yrn, k2 tog, k1, p10, k2, yfwd, k2 tog, k1.
2nd row Sl1, k2, yfwd, k2 tog, (k2, k2 tog, yfwd) twice, k3, yfwd, k2.
3rd row Yrn, k2 tog, k1, p11, k2, yrn, k2 tog, k1.
4th row Sl1, k2, yfwd, k2 tog, k1, k2 tog, yfwd, k2, k2 tog, yfwd, k5, yfwd, k2.
5th row Yrn, k2 tog, k1, p12, k2, yfwd, k2 tog, k1.
6th row Sl1, k2, yfwd, (k2 tog) twice, yfwd, k2, k2 tog, yfwd, k3, yfwd, k2 tog, k2, yfwd, k2.
7th row Yrn, k2 tog, k1, p13, k2, yfwd, k2 tog, k1.
8th row Sl1, k2, yfwd, k2 tog, k3, k2 tog, yfwd, k3, (yfwd, k2 tog) twice, k2, yfwd, k2.
9th row Yrn, k2 tog, k1, p14, k2, yfwd, k2 tog, k1.
10th row Sl1, k2, yfwd, k2 tog, k2, k2 tog, yfwd, k3, (yfwd, k2 tog) 3 times, k2, yfwd, k2.
11th row Yrn, k2 tog, k1, p15, k2, yfwd, k2 tog, k1.
12th row Sl1, k2, yfwd, k2 tog, k1, k2 tog, yfwd, k1, yfwd, sl1, k1, psso, k2, (yfwd, k2 tog) twice, k1, k2 tog, yfwd, k2 tog, k1.
13th row As 9th row.
14th row Sl1, k2, yfwd, (k2 tog) twice, yfwd, k3, yfwd, sl1, k1, psso, k2,

yfwd, k2 tog, k1, k2 tog, yfwd, k2 tog, k1.

15th row   As 7th row.

16th row   Sl1, k2, yfwd, k2 tog, k3, k2 tog, yfwd, k1, yfwd, sl1, k1, psso, k3, k2 tog, yfwd, k2 tog, k1.

17th row   As 5th row.

18th row   Sl1, k2, yfwd, k2 tog, k2, k2 tog, yfwd, k3, yfwd, sl1, k1, psso, k1, k2 tog, yfwd, k2 tog, k1.

19th row   As 3rd row.

20th row   Sl1, k2, yfwd, k2 tog, k1, k2 tog, yfwd, k2, k2 tog, yfwd, k1, yfwd, sl1, k2 tog, psso, yfwd, k2 tog, k1.

21st row   As 1st row.

22nd row   Sl1, k2, yfwd, (k2 tog) twice, k2, k2 tog, yfwd, k3, yfwd, k1, yfwd, k2 tog, k1 (*18 sts*).

These 22 rows form the pattern. Repeat them until work fits, unstretched, along width of sheet or all round pillowslip opening. Cast off.

To complete

Sew neatly to sheet edge or pillowslip opening. On pillowslip opening, join the cast-on edge to the cast-off edge.

41   Detail of knitted bedlinen edging, pattern 12

13 Alternative linen edgings

Materials
These will be similar to the linen edging requirements listed above for pattern 12.

Measurements
The fan pattern edging is 5 cm (2 in) wide.
The clover pattern edging is 6 cm (2½ in) wide.
The length of the edging is optional.

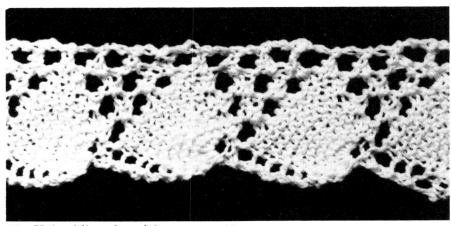

42 *Knitted linen fan edging, pattern 13*

To make fan edging
Cast on 14 sts.

1st row Sl1, (yrn) twice, k2 tog, k9, yrn, p2 tog.
2nd row K13, p1, k1.
3rd row Sl1, k12, yrn, p2 tog.
4th row K15.
5th row Sl1, *(yrn) twice, k2 tog; rep from * once more, k8, yrn, p2 tog.
6th row K12, p1, k2, p1, k1.
7th row Sl1, k14, yrn, p2 tog.
8th row K17.
9th row Sl1, *(yrn) twice, k2 tog; rep from * twice more, k8, yrn, p2 tog.
10th row K12, p1, (k2, p1) twice, k1.
11th row Sl1, k17, yrn, p2 tog.
12th row K20.
13th row K2 tog, *(yrn) twice, k2 tog; rep from * 3 times more, k8, yrn, p2 tog.
14th row K12, p1, (k2, p1) 3 times, k1.
15th row Sl1, k12, *insert right-hand needle point through the 2nd st on

left-hand needle and lift the st over the first st and off the needle; rep from
* until 9 sts have been lifted over the same st, k1.

16th row   K14.

These 16 rows form the pattern. Repeat them until the strip is the required
length.

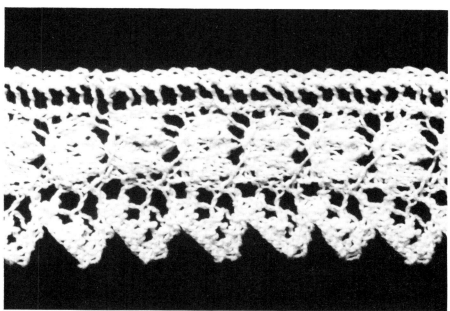

43   Knitted linen clover edging, pattern 13

To make clover pattern edging

Cast on 12 sts.

1st row   Sl1, k2 tog, (yrn) twice, k2 tog, yrn, k1, yrn, (k1, p1, k1) all in
next st, (yfwd, k1) twice, (yrn) twice, k2 tog, k1.

2nd row   K3, p1, k1, p9, k2, p1, k2.

3rd row   Sl1, k2 tog, (yrn) twice, k2 tog, (yfwd, k3) 3 times, yfwd, *k1,
(yrn) twice; rep from * once more, k2 tog, k1.

4th row   K3, p1, k2, p1, k1, p5, p3 tog, p5, k2, p1, k2.

5th row   Sl1, k2 tog, (yrn) twice, k2 tog, (yrn, sl1, k1, psso, k1, k2 tog,
yrn, k1) twice, * (yrn) twice, k2 tog; rep from * twice more, k1.

6th row   K3, (p1, k2) twice, p1, k1, (p2 tog, p1) 3 times, p2 tog, p2, p1,
k2.

7th row   Sl1, k2 tog, (yrn) twice, k2 tog, yrn, sl1, k2 tog, psso, k1, sl1, k2
tog, psso, k11.

8th row   Cast off 6 sts loosely (1 st now on right-hand needle), k4, p3 tog,
k3, p1, k2).

These 8 rows form the pattern. Repeat them until the strip is the required
length.

14 Pram or cot cover

44 *Leaf pattern pram or cot cover, pattern 14*

Generations of babies have been treated to coverlets similar to this one. The four decorative raised leaves tend to make the casual viewer assume that all the patterns are alike but closer inspection will usually reveal small differences. Before patterns were printed they were passed on by knitters who simply copied them or the directions were handed on by word of mouth. It is easy to see how small alterations occurred, albeit unintentionally.

This particular example is worked in an angora-look yarn. The yarn is very soft, and although the borders here have been hand-knitted, the edges could be covered in satin ribbon.

Materials

19 balls (20 g) Twilley Bobtail, angora-look
Pair 3¾ mm knitting needles

Measurements

83 cm (33 in) wide; 105 cm (43 in) long, including borders

Tension

Each square measures 12.5 cm (5 in) along each side.

Abbreviation

M1   make 1 st by working yrn.

To make
The square   Make 48 pieces.

Cast on 2 sts.

1st row   K1, m1, k1.

2nd row and foll alt rows to 6th row   P.

3rd row   (K1, m1) twice, k1.

5th row   (K1, m1) 4 times, k1.

7th row   K1, m1, p1, k2, m1, k1, m1, k2, p1, m1, k1.

8th row   P2, k1, p7, k1, p2.

9th row   K1, m1, p2, k3, m1, k1, m1, k3, p2, m1, k1.

10th row   P2, k2, p9, k2, p2.

11th row   K1, m1, p3, k4, m1, k1, m1, k4, p3, m1, k1.

12th row   P2, k3, p11, k3, p2.

13th row   K1, m1, p4, k5, m1, k1, m1, k5, p4, m1, k1.

14th row   P2, k4, p13, k4, p2.

15th row   K1, m1, p5, k6, m1, k1, m1, k6, p5, m1, k1.

16th row   P2, k5, p15, k5, p2.

17th row   K1, m1, p6, sl1, k1, psso, k11, k2 tog, p6, m1, k1.

18th row   P2, k6, p13, k6, p2.

19th row   K1, m1, p to centre leaf panel, sl1, k1, psso, k to last 2 sts of leaf panel, k2 tog, p to last st, m1, k1.

20th row   P the k and m sts and k the p sts of the previous row.

Repeat the last 2 rows 4 times.

29th row   K1, m1, p12, sl1, k2 tog, psso, p12, m1, k1.

30th row   P to end.

31st row   K to end inc 1 st at both end of the row (*31 sts*).

32nd and 33rd rows   As 30th row.

34th row   K2 tog, *m1, k2 tog; rep from * to last 3 sts, m1, k3 tog.

35th row   P to end.

36th row   P to end, dec 1 st at both ends of row.

37th row   K to end.

38th row   As 36th row.

39th row   P to end.

Repeat 34th to 39th rows 3 times, then 34th to 37th rows once only.

Purl remaining 3 sts together and fasten off.

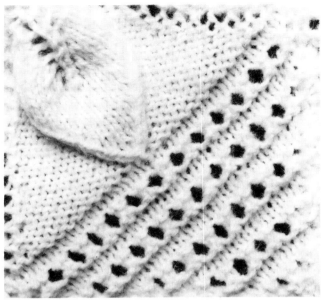

45   *Detail of leaf pattern square, pattern 14*

To make up

Placing the leaf points together, join four sections into a larger square. When all twelve large squares have been completed, join these together in four strips of three large squares. Mattress seam, with the right side of the work facing, is the most suitable for sewing these squares together.

The border

With right side of work facing, using $3\frac{3}{4}$ mm needles, pick up and knit 171 sts evenly along the length of the side edge. Work 1 row moss stitch, then continue in moss stitch, *at the same time* increasing 1 st at both ends of every row, until border measures 4 cm ($1\frac{1}{2}$ in). Cast off. Work the remaining long border in the same way.

The width borders are worked in the same way, but picking up and knitting 129 sts only, before working and increasing for the border.

With right side of work facing, mitre the corners by sewing together with a flat seam, taking just the edge stitch from each side and drawing these together very gently to avoid a bulky seam.

15 Lace curtains or screen

46 *Knitted lacy curtains, pattern 15*

Creating handmade curtains from your own handworked fabric could be considered quite a challenge; however, when the cloth is assembled from strips of knitting the possibilities are fascinating and the task is altogether easier.

This example is made with an insertion pattern through the centre, with the same pattern having an added point border for the outer strips. The curtains here are intended for small cottage-type windows, but by adding more insertion strips before sewing on those with borders the curtains can be any width you require, and, of course, they may be knitted to any length.

To use this idea as a screen, add at least 5 cm (2 in) to the top and bottom, so that the ends can be sewn into a channel for a piece of dowelling to be inserted. Curtains could also be hung onto dowelling rod at the top, or, if preferred, separate loops could be worked for the rod to pass through.

Materials
7 balls (50 g) Twilley Stalite No 3 cotton
Pair 5 mm knitting needles

Measurements
The quantities listed above will provide two curtains, each 56 cm (22 in) wide, 86 cm (34 in) long.

Tension
Each pattern repeat measures 15 cm (6 in) wide and 8.5 cm (3½ in) deep.

To make the border strips Make four pieces alike.
With 5 mm needles, cast on 33 sts loosely.
1st row K1, yrn, p2 tog, *k11, k2 tog, yrn twice to make 2 sts, k2 tog, k10* yrn, p2 tog, k1, yfwd, k2.
2nd row K4, yrn, p2 tog, *k12, p1 in second made st of 1st row, k12* yrn, p2 tog, k1.
3rd row K1, yrn, p2 tog, *k9, (k2 tog, yrn twice to make 2 sts, k2 tog) twice, k8, *yrn, p2 tog, k2, yfwd, k2.
4th row K5, yrn, p2 tog, *k10, p1 in second made st of previous row, k3, p1, k10, *yrn, p2 tog, k1.
5th row K1, yrn, p2 tog, *k7, (k2 tog, yrn twice to make 2 sts, k2 tog) 3 times, k6, *yrn, p2 tog, k3, yfwd, k2.
6th row K6, yrn, p2 tog, *k8, (p1 in second made st of previous row, k3) twice, p1 in second made st of previous row, k8, *yrn, p2 tog, k1.
7th row K1, yrn, p2 tog, *k5, (k2 tog, yrn twice to make 2 sts, k2 tog) 4 times, k4, *yrn, p2 tog, k2 tog, yrn twice to make 2 sts, k2, yfwd, k2.
8th row K6, p1 in second made st of previous row, k1, yrn, p2 tog, *k6, p1 in second made st of previous row, (k3, p1 in second made st of previous row) 3 times, k6, *yrn, p2 tog, k1.
9th row K1, yrn, p2 tog, *k3, (k2 tog, yrn twice to make 2 sts, k2 tog) 5 times, k2, *yrn, p2 tog, k8.

47   *Curtain strip with lace border, pattern 15*

10th row   Cast off 5 sts loosely (1 st now on right-hand needle), k2, yrn, p2 tog, *k4, p1 in second made st of previous row, (k3, p1 in second made st of previous row) 4 times, k4, *yrn, p2 tog, k1.

11th row   K1, yrn, p2 tog, *k5, (k2 tog, yrn twice to make 2 sts, k2 tog) 4 times, k4, *yrn, p2 tog, k1, yfwd, k2.

12th row   K4, yrn, p2 tog, *k6, p1, (k3, p1) 3 times, k6, *yrn, p2 tog, k1.

13th row   K1, yrn, p2 tog, *k7, (k2 tog, yrn twice to make 2 sts, k2 tog) 3 times, k6, *yrn, p2 tog, k2, yfwd, k2.

14th row   K5, yrn, p2 tog, *k8, p1, (k3, p1) twice, k8, *yrn, p2 tog, k1.

15th row   K1, yrn, p2 tog, *k9, (k2 tog, yrn twice to make 2 sts, k2 tog) twice, k8, *yrn, p2 tog, k3, yfwd, k2.

16th row   K6, yrn, p2 tog, *k10, p1, k3, p1, k10, *yrn, p2 tog, k1.

17th row   K1, yrn, p2 tog, *k11, k2 tog, yrn twice to make 2 sts, k2 tog, k10, *yrn, p2 tog, k2 tog, yrn twice to make 2 sts, k2, yfwd, k2.

18th row   K6, p1, k1, yrn, p2 tog, *k12, p1, k12, *yrn, p2 tog, k1.

19th row   K1, yrn, p2 tog, *k2, k2 tog, yrn twice to make 2 sts, k2 tog, k13, k2 tog, yrn twice to make 2 sts, k2 tog, k2, *yrn, p2 tog, k8.

20th row   Cast off 5 sts loosely (1 st now on right-hand needle), k2, yrn, p2 tog, *k4, p1 in second made st of previous row, k16, p1 in second made st of previous row, k3, *yrn, p2 tog, k1.

These 20 rows form the pattern including the outer borders. Repeat them until the curtains are 56 cm (22 in) long, ending after nearest 20th pattern row. Cast off loosely.

To make the insertion strips   Make two pieces.

These are simply the strips as given above without the borders. Cast on 25 sts and work in pattern as above, working only the pattern as it forms between * and * on every row.

Continue with the pattern until the strip is exactly the same number of rows as the outer pieces. Cast off.

To make up

With right side facing, join the strips with a flat seam so that, when hanging, the curtains appear to be in one continuous width.

To make hanging loops, cast on 9 sts. Cast off. Join these tiny cords into a circle and sew them at intervals to top of curtain. These loops will serve for narrow dowelling. Should larger-diameter rods be used, cast on more stitches (do not knit the stitches but cast them off immediately).

If the curtains are to be used as a screen, allow a little more yarn and work an extra 10 cm (4 in) before casting off. Fold the extra fabric to the wrong side of the work and slip stitch hem in place.

16 Leaf pattern cushion cover

48   *Leaf pattern knitted cushion cover, pattern 16*

Any of the square patterned bedspreads will lend themselves to being adapted for cushion covers. The motif for pattern 3 has been chosen for this cover and it has a plain stocking-stitch back. Using the quantities as a guide, you could make quite a collection of these attractive cushions, to complement the bedspread itself, or for the adornment of living-room chairs.

The yarn used and the close knitting will give many years of hard wear.

Materials

6 hanks (100 g) Twilley Handicraft No 1 cotton
Pair $3\frac{3}{4}$ mm knitting needles
40 cm (16 in) zip fastener

Measurements

46 cm (18 in) along each side edge

Tension

22 sts and 30 rows to 10 cm (4 in) measured over stocking stitch

To make

For the front of this cover, make four squares following the pattern instructions for the leaf bedspread pattern 3, page 34.

The back

With $3\frac{3}{4}$ mm needles, cast on 100 sts.
Beginning with a knit row, continue in stocking stitch until work measures 46 cm (18 in), ending after a purl row. Cast off.

To make up

Join the four squares into one large square with the leaves to the centre as on the bedspread. Place the right side of this square to the knit side of the stocking-stitch back and seam with back stitch round three of the sides and 2.5 cm (1 in) into the fourth side. Turn the cover to the right side and insert the zip fastener.

The crochet patterns

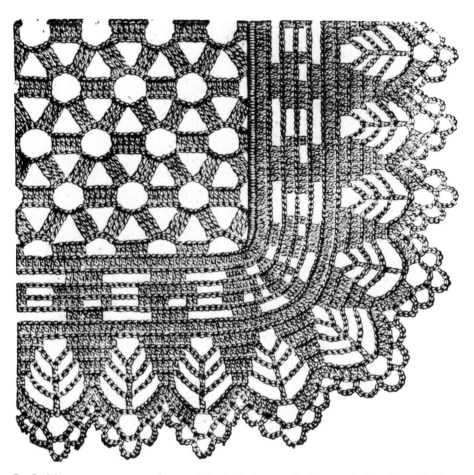

In fashion garments crochet, unlike knitting, only has periods of popularity, but for household articles it has permanent pride of place. As a craft it has many advantages. At its finest it imitates beautiful lace, at its thickest it can be used for floor rugs, and between these two extremes can be found a huge assortment of stitch patterns which, for the most part, lie wonderfully flat. Added to this is the bonus that, once acquired, the skill of crochet is tremendously fast.

Many of the items shown in this section have a traditional background. None of them is particularly grand in conception, so any one item is as suitable for the novice to work as the experienced worker. Wherever possible they have been revived in the piece-by-piece method, so that the small sections may be easily carried about.

1 Fine lace bedspread

The squares of this bedspread are relatively simple to work. However, the beginner to crochet may find the yarn very fine to use. It is suggested that the square is practised in a thicker yarn before beginning the fine squares. The more experienced craftswoman will find no problem and this bedspread has one great advantage: the squares are joined in the working.

The quantity of yarn suggested covers the making of the squares only; should you decide to add a fringe, add a few extra balls for this purpose. Unfringed, the lace makes a delicate window screen or a handsome tablecloth for special occasions (see page 51).

Materials
36 balls (20 g) Twilley Twenty Crochet Cotton No 20
1.5 mm crochet hook

Measurements
Width, 169 cm (68¾ in); length, 221 cm (89¼ in)

Tension
Each small square measures 13 cm (5¼ in) along each side.

To make
First motif
Make 8 ch and join into a ring with sl st.

1st round　Work 16 dc into ring and join with sl st to 1st dc.

2nd round　1 dc in same st, *7 ch, miss 3 dc, 1 dc in next dc; rep from * twice, 7 ch, sl st in 1st dc.

3rd round　*(1 dc, 1 htr, 2 tr, 3 dtr, 2 tr, 1 htr, 1 dc) all in next 7-ch sp; rep from * 3 times, sl st in 1st dc.

4th round　Sl st to centre dtr, 1 dc in same st, *7 ch, miss 2 sts, (leaving last loop of each st on hook work 1 tr in next st, miss 4 sts, 1 tr in next st, yrh and draw through all 3 loops) – cluster worked – 7 ch, miss 2 sts, 1 dc in centre dtr; rep from * 3 times, omitting 1 dc at end of last rep, sl st in 1st dc.

5th round　3 ch, (1 tr, 3 ch, 2 tr) in same st, *3 ch, 3 tr in next 7-ch sp, 1 tr in cluster, 3 tr in next 7-ch sp, 3 ch, (2 tr, 3 ch, 2 tr) in next dc; rep from * 3 times, omitting the (2 tr, 3 ch, 2 tr) group at end of last rep, sl st to top of 3 ch.

6th round　Sl st to 3-ch sp, (3 ch, 1 tr, 3 ch, 2 tr) in same sp, *5 ch, miss next sp and next tr, 1 tr in each of next 5 tr, 5 ch, miss next sp, (2 tr, 3 ch, 2 tr) in next 3-ch sp; rep from * 3 times, omitting (2 tr, 3 ch, 2 tr) group at end of last rep, sl st to top of 3 ch.

7th round　Sl st to 3-ch sp, 3 ch, (2 tr, 3 ch, 3 tr) in same sp, *7 ch, miss

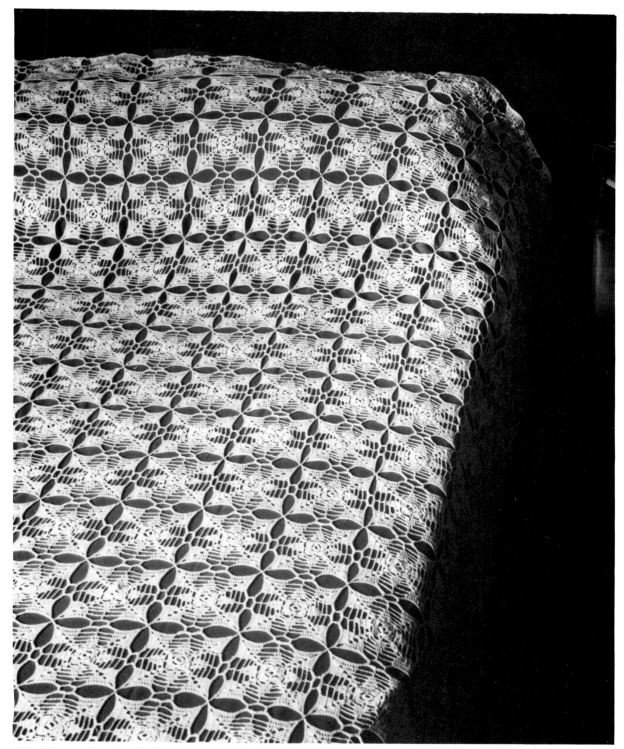

49 *Fine crochet lace bedspread, pattern 1*

next sp and next tr, 1 tr in each of next 3 tr, 7 ch, (3 tr, 3 ch, 3 tr) in next 3-ch sp; rep from * 3 times, omitting (3 tr, 3 ch, 3 tr) at end of last rep, sl st to top of 3 ch.

8th round 3 ch, *1 tr in each of next 2 tr, (3 tr, 3 ch, 3 tr) in 3-ch sp, 1 tr in each of next 3 tr, 9 ch, miss 1 tr, 1 tr in next tr, 9 ch, 1 tr in next tr; rep from * 3 times, omitting 1 tr at end of last rep, sl st to top of 3 ch.

9th round 3 ch, *1 tr in each of next 5 sts, (3 dtr, 5 ch, 3 dtr) in 3-ch sp, 1 tr in each of next 6 tr, 9 ch, 1 tr in next tr, 9 ch, 1 tr in next tr; rep from * 3 times, omitting 1 tr at end of last rep, sl st to top of 3 ch.

10th round 1 dc in same st, *1 dc in each of next 8 sts, 3 dc in 5-ch sp, 5 ch, sl st in last dc – corner picot worked – 2 dc in same ch sp, 1 dc in each of next 9 sts, (6 dc in next 9-ch sp, 3 ch, sl st in last dc – side picot worked – 5 dc in same ch-sp) twice, 1 dc in next tr; rep from * 3 times, omitting 1 dc at end of last rep, sl st to 1st dc. Fasten off.

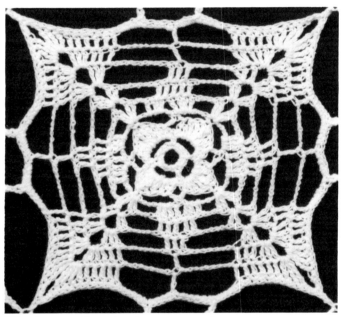

50 *Square of crochet lace, pattern 1*

Second motif

Work as first motif to the end of the 9th round.

10th (joining) round 1 dc in same st, *1 dc in each of next 8 sts, 3 dc in 5-ch sp, 2 ch, sl st to corner picot of first motif, 2 ch, sl st in last dc on second motif, 2 dc in same ch sp, 1 dc in each of next 9 sts, *(6 dc in 9-ch sp, 1 ch, sl st in side picot of first motif, 1 ch, sl st in last dc of second motif, 5 dc in same ch sp) twice, 1 dc in next st; rep from * to * once, (6 dc, 1 side picot, 5 dc) in same ch sp; rep the bracketed section of 10th round of first motif once, 1 dc in next tr; rep from * of 10th round of first motif twice, omitting 1 dc at end of last rep, sl st to 1st dc. Fasten off. Continue in this way until a strip of 13 squares has been completed. Join next motif to side of first motif then continue joining motifs to previous motif and to side of previous motif strip until 17 strips have been completed.

To complete

If a fringe is required, cut supply of yarn into 25 cm (10 in) lengths. Using six strands together, fold in half, using hook, draw the doubled loops through, wrap ends round hook and draw through the loops; pull to secure. Repeat this action at intervals along the side edges.

The same motif can be used to make a tablecloth. Decide on the finished size of the tablecloth and from this estimate the number of motifs required (see page 9).

51   Fine crochet lace bedspread in use as a tablecloth, pattern 1

2 Fan swirl bedspread

52 Crochet lace swirl strip bedspread, pattern 2

The name given to this pattern derives from the fan shape which alternates from side to side of the strips. It is easily and rapidly worked and as it is made in sections it is readily transportable. The yarn used for this example is quite thick, producing a richly-textured quilt – a finer yarn will give a lace effect; it is worth experimenting with different yarns to see which fabric best suits your requirements.

This particular design when worked in suitable yarn will also make a beautiful christening shawl for a baby. Similarly, made in shorter strips it can be adapted for use as a pram or cot cover.

Materials
33 hanks (100 g) Twilley Handicraft No 1 cotton
4 mm crochet hook

Measurements
Width, 204 cm (81 in); length, 228 cm (90 in)

Tension
To obtain these measurements each strip should measure 17 cm ($6\frac{3}{4}$ in) wide.

To make
First strip
Make 28 ch.

1st row   1 dc in 8th ch from hook, 3 ch, miss 3 ch, 1 dc in next ch, turn.

2nd row   3 ch, 4 tr in next sp, 1 tr in next dc, 4 tr in next sp, turn.

3rd row   4 ch, 1 tr in next tr, (2 ch, miss 1 tr, 1 tr in next tr) 4 times, 2 ch, 1 tr in last dc of first row, miss 2 base ch, sl st in next base ch st, 1 ch, miss 1 base ch st, sl st in next base ch st, turn.

4th row   (1 tr in next tr, 2 tr in next sp) 5 times, 1 tr in next tr, 1 tr in last sp, 1 tr in 3rd ch, turn.

5th row   3 ch, (1 tr in next tr, 1 ch, miss 1 tr) 5 times, (1 tr in next tr, 2 ch, miss 1 tr) 3 times, 1 tr in next tr, miss 2 base ch sts, sl st in next base ch st, turn.

6th row   3 ch, (miss next sp, 1 dc in next tr, 3 ch) twice, miss next sp, 1 dc in next tr, turn.

7th row   Miss next sp, 1 tr in next dc, 2 tr in next sp, 1 tr in next dc, 3 tr in next sp, miss 1 base ch st, sl st in next base ch st, 2 ch, miss 1 base ch st, sl st in next base ch st, turn.

8th row   2 ch, miss next tr (1 tr in next tr, 2 ch) 6 times, sl st in next sp on previous motif, turn.

9th row   (2 tr in next sp, 1 tr in next tr) 6 times, 2 tr in next sp, 1 tr in sl st, miss 1 base ch st, sl st in next base ch st, 2 ch, miss 1 base ch st, sl st in last base ch st, turn.

10th row   2 ch, (miss 1 tr, 1 tr in next tr, 3 ch) 3 times, (miss 1 tr, 1 tr in next tr, 2 ch) 7 times, miss 1 tr, 1 tr in next st, sl st in next sp on previous motif, turn.

11th row   3 ch, (miss next sp, 1 dc in next tr, 3 ch) twice, miss next sp, 1 dc in next tr, turn.

12th row   Miss next sp, 1 tr in next dc, 2 tr in next sp, 1 tr in next dc, 3 tr in next sp, sl st in sp on previous motif, 1 ch, sl st in next sp on previous motif, turn.

13th row   2 ch, miss next tr, (1 tr in next tr, 2 ch) 6 times, sl st in next sp on previous motif, 1 ch, sl st in next tr on previous motif, turn.

14th row   (2 tr in next sp, 1 tr in next tr) 6 times, 2 tr in next sp, 1 tr in next st, sl st in next sp on previous motif, 1 ch, sl st in last sp on previous motif, turn.

53 *Lace swirl strip pattern, pattern 2*

15th row   2 ch, (miss 1 tr, 1 tr in next tr, 3 ch) 3 times, (miss 1 tr, 1 tr in next tr, 2 ch) 7 times, miss 1 tr, 1 tr in next st, sl st in next sp on previous motif, turn.

16th row   3 ch, (miss next sp, 1 dc in next tr, 3 ch) twice, miss next sp, 1 dc in next tr, turn.

17th row   Miss next sp, 1 tr in next dc, 2 tr in next sp, 1 tr in next dc, 3 tr in next sp, sl st in next tr on previous motif, 1 ch, sl st in next sp on previous motif, turn.

18th row   2 ch, miss next tr, (1 tr in next tr, 2 ch) 6 times, sl st in next sp on previous motif, 1 ch, sl st in next sp on previous motif, turn.

19th row (2 tr in next sp, 1 tr in next tr) 6 times, 2 tr in next sp, 1 tr in next st, sl st in next tr on previous motif, 1 ch, sl st in next sp on previous motif, turn.

Repeat 15th to 19th rows for pattern until strip measures approx 228 cm (90 in) ending after nearest 15th row.

Continue along 15th row thus: (4 tr in next sp) 3 times, 3 ch, turn.

Next row 3 ch, (miss 1 tr, 1 tr in next tr, 1 ch) 6 times, sl st in 1st sp on previous motif. Fasten off.

Make 11 more strips in the same way.

To complete

With right side facing, join in yarn at one corner and work a row of double crochet along all edges, working in treble between motifs to straighten the edges. Fasten off.

The strips may be sewn together, but a crochet join is faster and neater. Place two strips together, right sides facing, insert hook through back loop only of each edge stitch, draw loop through, yarn round hook and through all loops on hook. Continue in this way to end of strip.

The border

A narrow border was added to complement the strip pattern and this was worked directly on to the fabric. There are many suitable borders that may be worked and sewn to the edges but care should be taken to avoid very wide borders since these might detract from the main pattern.

To make

Join yarn in corner st, 4 ch, (1 tr, 1 ch) twice in same st, 1 tr in same st, *miss 3 sts, 1 tr in next st, (1 ch, 1 tr) 3 times in same st; rep from * to end, sl st in 3rd of 4 ch. Fasten off.

3 Octagon and square bedspread

The motifs that form this bedspread are joined in such a way as to leave natural breaks in the fabric, giving an opportunity to show off your favourite throwover quilt or a new fabric shade that will set it off and tie in with the general colour scheme.

While this design is not recommended for use as a tablecloth, the octagon motifs would serve very well as place mats, and the basic pattern can be repeated to form a large centre mat.

54   *Crochet octagon and square bedspread, pattern 3*

Materials
34 balls (50 g) Twilley Stalite No 3 cotton
3.5 mm crochet hook

Measurements
Width 162 cm (64 in); length 204 cm (80 in)

Tension
To obtain these measurements the octagon motifs should have a diameter
of 20 cm (8 in) and the filler square motifs should be 6 cm (2½ in) square.

Special abbreviation
Dtrf   double treble front worked thus: bring hook to front of work and
inserting hook from right to left work a double treble round the stem of the
next treble.

To make
Octagon motif   Make a total of 60 pieces.

Make 5 ch and join into a ring with sl st into first ch.

1st round   5 ch, (1 tr in ring, 2 ch), 7 times, sl st in 3rd of 5 ch. Do not
turn.

2nd round   Sl st in 2-ch sp, 3 ch, 4 tr in same sp, 1 ch, (5 tr in next sp,
1 ch) 7 times, sl st in 3rd ch.

3rd round   3 ch, (2 tr in next tr, work dtrf round next tr, 2 tr in next tr,
1 tr in next tr, 1 ch, 1 tr in next tr) 8 times, omitting 1 tr in next tr at end
of last rep, sl st in 3rd ch.

4th round   3 ch, (1 tr in each of next 2 tr, 1 dtrf round next st, 1 tr in each
of next 3 tr, 2 ch, 1 tr in next tr) 8 times, omitting 1 tr in next tr at end of
last rep, sl st in top of 3 ch.

5th and 6th rounds   3 ch, (1 tr in each of next 2 tr, 1 dtrf round dtrf, 1 tr in
each of next 3 tr, 3 ch, 1 tr in next tr) 8 times, omitting 1 tr in next tr at
end of last rep, sl st in top of 3 ch.

7th round   3 ch, (1 tr in next tr, 2 tr in next tr, 1 dtrf round dtrf, 2 tr in
next tr, 1 tr in each of next 2 tr, 3 ch, 1 tr in next tr) 8 times, omitting 1 tr
in next tr at end of last rep, sl st in top of 3 ch.

8th round   3 ch, (1 tr in each of next 2 tr, 2 tr in next tr, 1 dtrf round dtrf,
2 tr in next tr, 1 tr in each of next 3 tr, 3 ch, 1 tr in next tr) 8 times,
omitting 1 tr in next tr at end of last rep, sl st in top of 3 ch.

9th round   1 ch, 1 dc in top of 3 ch, (1 htr in each of next 2 tr, 1 tr in next
tr, 1 dtr in next tr, 1 dtrf round dtrf, 1 dtr in next tr, 1 tr in next tr, 1 htr,
in each of next 2 tr, 1 dc in next tr, 1 sl st in each of next 3 ch, 1 dc in next
tr) 8 times, omitting 1 dc in next tr at end of last rep, sl st in first ch.
Fasten off.

When working remaining octagon motifs, work to the end of the 8th round
and join thus:

9th round   1 dc in same st as sl st, 1 htr in each of next 2 tr, 1 tr in next tr,
1 dtr in next tr, 1 dtrf round next dtrf, sl st to top of dtrf of first motif, 1

55   Octagon and square motifs, pattern 3

dtr in tr on second motif, 1 tr in next tr, 1 htr in each of next 2 tr, 1 dc in next tr, 1 sl st in each of next 3 ch, 1 dc in next tr, 1 htr in each of next 2 tr, 1 tr in next tr, 1 dtrf round next dtrf, sl st to top of adjacent dtrf of first motif, then complete as remainder of 9th round of first motif.

Continue in this way working remaining octagon motifs, joining as last motif was joined to the first motif, attaching on one, two or three sides as required to form 8 motifs across the width and 10 motifs along the length.

Filler motifs

Make 5 ch and join into a ring with sl st into first ch.

1st round   3 ch (stands as 1st tr), 3 tr into ring, (1 ch, 4 tr into ring) 3 times, 1 ch, join with sl st to top of 3 ch.

2nd round   Sl st along to first 1-ch sp, 3 ch (stands as 1st tr), (2 tr, 2 ch, 3 tr) all in 1-ch sp, (3 tr, 2 ch, 3 tr, all in next 1-ch sp) 3 times, join with sl st to top of 3 ch.

3rd round   Sl st along to next 2-ch sp, 3 ch, 2 tr, 1 ch, sl st in centre of 3 sl sts between two points of one octagon motif, 1 ch, 3 tr in same 2-ch sp, (3 tr between next two sets of 3 tr along one side, 3 tr, 1 ch, sl st in centre of 3 sl sts of adjacent octagon motif, 1 ch, 3 tr in next 2-ch sp) 3 times, 3 tr between next two sets of 3 tr along last side, join with sl st to top of 3 ch. Fasten off.

To complete

The bedspread may be embellished with tassels to make the outer edges of the octagons hang well, or the crochet may be lined with contrasting cloth.

4   Irish crochet granny squares bedspread

A truly old-fashioned 'patchwork' bedcover. The squares are frequently worked in colours, but the raised texture of the traditional stitch patterns gives lustre to the natural quality of pure cotton, and it looks exactly right in white.

The spread takes quite a large number of squares but they are very quickly made – why not work with a friend and enjoy watching the pile of squares grow?

Materials

33 hanks (100 g) Twilley Handicraft No 1 cotton
4 mm crochet hook

Measurements

Width, 167 cm (66 in); length, 228 cm (90 in) excluding border.

Tension

Each square should measure 15 cm (6 in) along each side to obtain the measurements stated above.

56 *Irish crochet granny squares bedspread, pattern 4*

1 Canterbury bell knitted bedspread. *Pattern 1*

2 Octagon pattern knitted bedspread. *Pattern 5*

3 Machine knitted bedspread. *Pattern 8*

4 Lace and moss pattern knitted tablecloth. *Pattern 9*

5 Lace swirl knitted table linen. *Pattern 10*

6 Knitted pleated tea cosy.
Pattern 11

7 Leaf pattern knitted cushion cover. *Pattern 16*

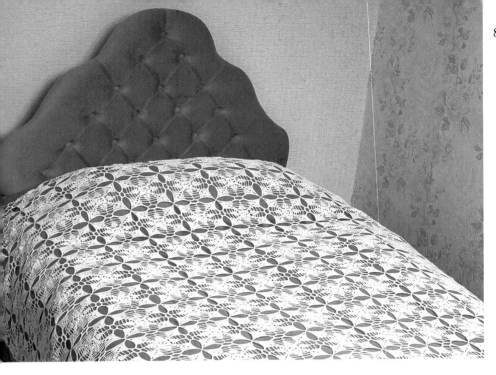

8 Fine lace crochet
bedspread. *Pattern 1*

9 Fine lace crochet used as
tablecloth. *Pattern 1*

10 Octagon and square crochet bedspread. *Pattern 3*

11 Crochet table linen. *Pattern 7*

12 Crochet tray cloth, full size. *Pattern 8*

57 *Irish crochet popcorn motif, pattern 4*

Popcorn motif Make 83 pieces.

Make 4 ch, join into ring with sl st.

1st round 3 ch, 11 tr into ring, join with sl st in top of 3 ch.

2nd round 3 ch, 5 tr between 3 ch and 1 tr on first round, (miss 3 tr, 6 tr between trs) 3 times, miss 3 tr, sl st in top of 3 ch.

3rd round 3 ch, 2 tr at base of 3 ch, (miss 3 tr, 6 tr between trs, miss 3 tr, 3 tr between trs) 3 times, miss 3 tr, 6 tr between trs, sl st in top of 3 ch.

4th round 3 ch, 2 tr between last and first groups at base of 3 ch, (miss 3 tr, 3 tr between trs, miss 3 tr, 6 tr between trs, miss 3 tr, 3 tr between trs) 3 times, miss 3 tr, 6 tr between trs, sl st in top of 3 ch.

5th round 3 ch, 4 tr between last and first groups at base of 3 ch, remove hook, insert hook into top of 3 ch, then into dropped loop and draw loop through, 3 ch, miss 3 tr, *(5 tr between trs, remove hook, insert hook into first of 5 tr, then into dropped loop and draw loop through – a popcorn made – 3 ch, miss 3 tr) twice, (1 popcorn, 3 ch, 1 popcorn) between trs, 3 ch, miss 3 tr, 1 popcorn between trs, 3 ch, miss 3 tr; rep from * twice more, (1 popcorn between trs, 3 ch, miss 3 tr) twice, (1 popcorn, 3 ch, 1 popcorn) between trs, 3 ch, miss 3 tr, sl st in top of 3 ch.

6th round   3 ch, 2 tr in previous 3-ch sp, *(3 tr in next 3-ch sp) 3 times, 6 tr in next sp, 3 tr in next sp; rep from * twice more, (3 tr in next sp) 3 times, 6 tr in next sp, sl st in top of 3 ch. Fasten off.

58   *Irish crochet rose motif, pattern 4*

Rose motif   Make 82 pieces.

Make 4 ch and join into ring with sl st.

1st round   *2 ch, 4 tr into ring, sl st into ring; rep from * 3 times more.

2nd round   Sl st in back of 3rd tr, *keeping yarn in back of work, 4 ch, sl st in 3rd tr of next group; rep from * twice more, 4 ch, join with sl st to first sl st.

3rd round   Into each 4-ch loop work 1 sl st, 5 tr, 1 sl st, making four petals.

4th round   *6 ch, 1 sl st into back of sl st between petals; rep from * 3 times more.

5th round   3 ch, (2 tr, 3 ch, 3 tr) into same 6-ch loop, *1 ch, (3 tr, 3 ch, 3 tr) into next loop; rep from * twice more, 1 ch, join with sl st to 3rd of 3 ch.

6th round   3 ch, (2 tr, 3 ch, 3 tr) into same sp, *1 ch, 3 tr into 1-ch sp, 1 ch, (3 tr, 3 ch, 3 tr) into 3-ch sp; rep from * twice more, 1 ch, 3 tr into 1-ch sp, 1 ch, join with sl st to 3rd of 3 ch.

7th round   3 ch, (2 tr, 3 ch, 3 tr) into same sp, *(1 ch, 3 tr into 1-ch sp) twice, 1 ch, (3 tr, 3 ch, 3 tr) into 3-ch sp; rep from * twice more, (1 ch, 3 tr into 1-ch sp) twice, 1 ch, join with sl st to 3rd of 3 ch.

Work 2 more rounds in this way, repeating the sections in brackets (parentheses) 3 times more instead of twice. Fasten off.

To make up

Join the squares alternately, with 11 squares to the width and 15 squares to the length, noting that there will be a popcorn motif in each corner. This example was joined four squares at a time for ease of work, with right sides facing, and sewn through the back loops of the last rows. This method leaves a neat edging on the right side of the work.

5   Border for Irish crochet bedspread

59   *Border for Irish crochet bedspread, pattern 5*

The quantities given for the bedspread will be sufficient to make this narrow border, and the same size of crochet hook as that used for the squares will produce a suitable tension.

Join yarn in one corner of the completed bedspread.

1st round   *5 ch, miss 3 sts, 1 dc into next space between trs; rep from * all round outer edge, working an uneven number of dc to each side and turning the corners with 5 ch. Join to first st with sl st.

2nd round   3 ch (stands as 1st tr), 2 tr, 3 ch, 3 tr in next 5-ch loop, *1 dc in next 5-ch loop, 3 tr, 3 ch, 3 tr in next 5-ch loop; rep from * to end, working 1 dc in last loop. Join to 3rd of 3 ch with sl st. Fasten off.

6   Openwork tablecloth

This will add a touch of luxury for afternoon tea or provide a centre-piece at a dinner party if it is laid over a large cloth of a contrasting colour. Although it is made in one piece, this cloth is not heavy to work or to carry about in the making because a lightweight yarn is used to produce this lacy pattern.

The fabric hangs well, making it suitable for use as a window screen (see page 00). For really dedicated crochet workers there might also be the prospect of a bedspread in this design, simply adding on 18 ch for each extra repeat of the pattern for the added width. The amount of extra yarn required for a bedspread may be calculated from the quantities given for this size of tablecloth (see page 00).

Materials
13 balls (25 g) Twilley Lyscordet No 5 cotton
2 mm crochet hook

Measurements
91 cm (36 in) along each side edge, excluding border

Tension
Each repeat of pattern measures 8 cm (3 in) in width.

To make
Make 221 ch.

1st row   1 tr in 4th ch from hook, 1 tr in next ch, *(5 ch, miss 3 ch, 1 dc in next ch) 3 times, 5 ch, miss 3 ch, 1 tr in each of next 3 ch; rep from *11 times more, 5 ch, turn.

2nd row   *3 tr in next loop, (5 ch, 1 dc in next loop) twice, 5 ch, 3 tr in next loop, 2 ch; rep from * to end, ending 1 tr in 3rd of turning ch, 5 ch, turn.

3rd row   *1 tr in each of next 3 tr, 3 tr in next loop, 5 ch, 1 dc in next

60　Openwork crochet tablecloth, pattern 6

loop, 5 ch, 3 tr in next loop, 1 tr in each of next 3 tr, 2 ch; rep from * to end, ending 1 tr in 3rd of 5 ch, 5 ch, turn.

4th row　*1 tr in each of next 6 tr, 3 tr in next loop, 2 ch, 3 tr in next loop, 1 tr in each of next 6 tr, 2 ch; rep from * to end, ending 1 tr on 3rd of 5 ch, 1 ch, turn.

5th row　*1 dc in next sp, 5 ch, miss 3 tr, 1 tr in each of next 6 tr, 2 ch, 1 tr in each of next 6 tr, 5 ch; rep from * to end, ending 1 dc in last sp, 5 ch, turn.

6th row　1 dc in next loop, *5 ch, miss 3 tr, 1 tr in each of next 3 tr, 2 ch, 1 tr in each of 3 tr, (5 ch, 1 dc in next loop) twice; rep from * to end, omitting 5 ch and 1 dc at end of last rep, ending 2 ch, 1 tr in last dc, 5 ch, turn.

7th row　1 dc in next 2-ch loop, 5 ch, 1 dc in next loop, *5 ch, 3 tr in next 2-ch sp, (5 ch, 1 dc in next loop) 3 times; rep from * to end, omitting 5 ch and 1 dc at end of last rep, ending 2 ch, 1 tr in 3rd of 5 ch, 1 ch, turn.

8th row　1 dc in 2-ch loop, 5 ch, 1 dc in next loop, *5 ch, 3 tr in next loop, 2 ch, 3 tr in next loop, (5 ch, 1 dc in next loop) twice; rep from * to end, ending 1 dc in same loop, 5 ch, turn.

9th row　1 dc in next loop, *5 ch, 3 tr in next loop, 1 tr in each of next 3 tr, 2 ch, 1 tr in each of next 3 tr, 3 tr in next loop, 5 ch, 1 dc in next loop; rep from * to end, ending 2 ch, 1 tr in last dc, 5 ch, turn.

10th row　*3 tr in next 5-ch loop, 1 tr in each of next 6 tr, 2 ch, 1 tr in each of next 6 tr, 3 tr in next loop, 2 ch; rep from * to end, ending 1 tr in 3rd of 5 ch, 5 ch, turn.

61 *Crochet tablecloth, pattern 6, used as a window screen*

11th row   *1 tr in each of next 6 tr, 5 ch, 1 dc in next sp, 5 ch, miss 3 tr, 1 tr in each of next 6 tr, 2 ch; rep from * to end, ending 1 tr in 3rd of 5 ch, 5 ch, turn.

12th row   *1 tr in each of 3 tr, (5 ch, 1 dc in next loop) twice, 5 ch, miss 3 tr, 1 tr in each of next 3 tr, 2 ch; rep from * to end, ending 1 tr in 3rd of 5 ch, 5 ch, turn.

13th row   2 tr in next sp, *(5 ch, 1 dc in next loop) 3 times, 5 ch, 3 tr in next sp; rep from * to end, ending 5 ch, turn.

The 2nd to 13th rows form the pattern. Continue in pattern until work measures 91 cm (36 in) ending after nearest 13th pattern row, on the *last* 13th row, work 3 ch instead of 5 ch between the 3-tr groups and omit the 5 ch at the end of the last row. Do not fasten off.

Continue with the border thus:

The border (worked in rounds)

1st round Work 1 round dc all round outer edge, working a multiple of 4 sts. Join with sl st to first dc.

2nd round 3 ch, 1 tr in same place as sl st, 4 ch, 2 tr in same place, *3 ch, miss 3 dc, 2 tr in next dc; rep from * along side, into next corner work 2 tr, 4 ch, 2 tr. Continue in this way all round work, ending 3 ch, sl st in 3rd of 3 ch.

3rd round Sl st to next corner loop, 1 ch, into each corner loop work 4 dc, into each tr work 1 dc, into each 3-ch sp work 3 dc; join with sl st to 1st ch.

4th round Sl st to centre of corner loop, 8 ch, 1 tr in same place as last sl st, *5 ch, miss 3 dc, 1 dc in next dc; rep from * along sides, 1 tr, 5 ch, and 1 tr into centre dc of each corner, join with sl st into 3rd of 8 ch.

5th round Sl st into corner loop, 3 ch, leaving last loop on hook, make 2 tr in same loop, yrh and draw through all loops – cluster made – (5 ch, make 3-tr clusters) 4 times in same loop, *3 ch, miss next loop, 1 dc in next loop, 5 ch, 1 dc in next loop, 3 ch, miss next loop, work three 3-tr clusters with 5 ch between in next loop; rep from * along sides, into each corner loop work 5 3-tr clusters with 5 ch between, join with sl st to tip of first cluster. Fasten off.

To complete

The cloth may be pressed very lightly, preferably on a flat surface (not an ironing board). The border should be carefully blocked out with pins to retain its shape.

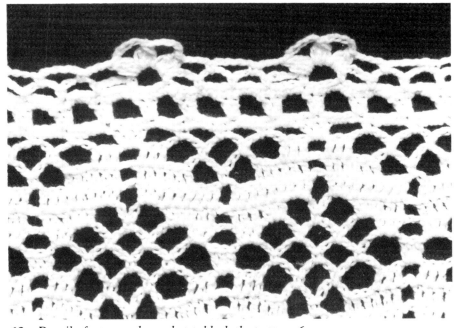

62   Detail of openwork crochet tablecloth, pattern 6

7 Table linen

63   Circular crochet table linen, pattern 7

The pattern for these place mats is repeated in the centre mat. It would also be suitable for a full-size circular tablecloth – it is simply a matter of repeating the motifs and joining them until they fit the size of cloth you wish to surround.

Materials

10 balls (25 g) Twilley Lyscordet No. 5 cotton
2 mm crochet hook
Small piece linen or cotton fabric

Measurements

Centre mat diameter 63 cm (25 in)
Place mat diameter 25 cm (10 in)
Coaster diameter 12.5 cm (5 in)

Tension

28 tr and 14 rows tr to 10 cm (4 in)

Note

1 ball cotton will make 4 coasters; 1 ball cotton will make 1 place mat; 5 balls will make the motifs for the centre mat.

The centre mat
To make first motif

Make 8 ch and join into ring with sl st.
1st round   9 ch, (1 dtr into ring, 5 ch) 7 times, join with sl st to 4th of 9 ch.
2nd round   8 dc in each 5-ch loop, sl st to first dc.
3rd round   3 ch, 1 tr in each dc to end, sl st in top of 3 ch.
4th round   4 ch, leaving last loop of each st on hook, work 1 dtr in each of next 2 tr, yrh and draw through all loops, *6 ch, miss next tr, leaving last loop on hook, work 1 dtr in each of next 3 tr, yrh and draw through all loops – 3-dtr cluster made; rep from * ending with 6 ch, sl st in top of first cluster.
5th round   8 dc in each 6-ch loop, sl st in first dc.
6th round   Sl st in next 2 dc, 3 ch, 1 tr in each of next 11 dc, *5ch, miss 4 dc, 1 tr in each of next 12 dc; rep from * ending 5 ch, sl st in top of 3 ch.
7th round   3 ch, 1 tr in each of next 11 tr, *5 ch, 1 dc in next loop, 5 ch, 1 tr in each of next 12 tr; rep from * ending 5 ch, 1 dc in next loop, 5 ch, sl st in top of 3 ch.
8th round   3 ch, 1 tr in each of next 11 tr, *(5 ch, 1 dc in next sp) twice, 5 ch, 1 tr in each of next 12 tr; rep from * ending sl st in top of 3 ch.
9th round   Sl st over next 2 tr, 3 ch, 1 tr in each of next 7 tr, *(5 ch, 1 dc in next loop) 3 times, 5 ch, miss next 2 tr, 1 tr in each of next 8 tr; rep from * ending sl st in top of 3 ch.
10th round   Sl st over next 2 tr, 3 ch, 1 tr in each of next 3 tr, *(5 ch, 1 dc in loop) 4 times, 5 ch, miss next 2 tr, 1 tr in each of next 4 tr; rep from * ending sl st in top of 3 ch. Fasten off.

To make second motif

Work as first motif to end of 9th round.
10th round   Sl st over next 2 tr, 3 ch, 1 tr in each of next 3 tr, *(5 ch, 1 dc

in next loop) 4 times, 5 ch, miss next 2 tr, 1 tr in each of next 4 tr; rep from * 5 times more, 2 ch, sl st to any last worked 5-ch loop on any of the 5-ch loop sections on previous motif, (2 ch, dc in next loop on second motif, 2 ch, sl st in next loop of previous motif) 4 times, 2 ch, miss next 2 tr, 1 tr in each of next 4 tr, (5 ch, 1 dc in next loop) 4 times, 5 ch, sl st in top of 3 ch. Fasten off.

Make five more motifs, joining adjacent sides as the second motif was joined to the first motif, into a circular shape, leaving 20 loops at the outer edge and 10 loops at the centre and joining the first and last motifs to join the circle.

Border

Rejoin yarn to any 2-ch space preceding the join of motifs.

1 dc in same sp, *1 dc in corresponding 2-ch sp following join on next motif, (5 ch, 1 dc in next loop) 20 times, 5 ch, 1 dc in 2-ch sp preceding the join; rep from * ending sl st in first dc.

2nd round 7 dc in each 5-ch sp, sl st in first dc.

3rd round Sl st over next 2 dc, 4 ch, leaving last loop on hook, work 1 dtr in each of next 2 dc, yrh and draw through all loops,* 6 ch, miss next 4 dc, work 3-dtr cluster over next 3 dc; rep from * to end, ending sl st in top of first 3-dtr cluster.

4th round In each 6-ch sp, work 3 dc, 5 ch, sl st in first of 5 ch to form picot, 3 dc, join with sl st to first dc. Fasten off.

To complete

Lay the piece of fabric flat on a table. Place the ring of motifs on the fabric and gently move the circle until the centre is exactly equidistant between the motifs. Pin the sections in place, then neatly hem around the inner edge of the crochet to attach it to the cloth. Turn the work to the wrong side and carefully cut away the excess cloth close to the hemstitch join, leaving approximately 0.5 cm ($\frac{1}{4}$ in) rebate. Turn in this raw edge and neatly hem in place.

The place mats   Make four.
To make

Work as pattern instructions for first motif of centre mat until 10th round has been completed. Do not fasten off.

Border

1st round Sl st to centre of next 4 tr, 5 ch, *dc in next 5-ch loop, 5 ch, rep from * to next 4 tr, 1 dc between centre of next 4 tr, 5 ch. Continue in this way all round, sl st to first sl st.

2nd round 7 dc in each 5-ch sp to end, join with sl st to first dc.

3rd round Sl st over next 2 dc, 4 ch, 1 dtr in each of next 2 dc leaving last loop of each st on hook, yrh and draw through all loops; 6 ch, *3-dtr cluster in centre of next 7-dc group, 6 ch; rep from * to end, sl st to top of first dtr cluster.

4th round In each 6-ch sp, work 3 dc, 5 ch, sl st in first of 5 ch, to form picot, 3 dc, join with sl st to first dc. Fasten off.

64 *Place mat of crochet table linen, pattern 7*

The coasters Make four.

Work as pattern instructions for first motif of centre mat until the 5th round has been worked. Continue thus:
6th round Work as previous 6th round working 2 ch, make picot, 2 ch, between each set of 12 tr instread of 5 ch. Fasten off.

To complete

Pressing is recommended for these mats. The crochet sections should be blocked (i.e. pinned out into the correct shape) and pressed lightly under a damp cloth and left to dry out completely without being disturbed. This will retain the crispness of the lace. Before pressing the centre mat make sure that the fabric used in the centre of the crochet will withstand pressing; if not, take care to avoid that area.

8 Tray cloth

65 *Tray cloth of small crochet motifs, pattern 8*

This neat little cloth is made from very small motifs. Having established the motif it is very tempting to add more and more to make up a useful set of household linen that will wash and wear for years. The quantities are given for the items shown, but it is easy enough to see how many squares can be made from one ball. The number of balls needed for any other article you might wish to make from this pattern can then be calculated.

Materials
3 balls (25 g) Twilley Lyscordet No 5 cotton
2 mm crochet hook

To make
First motif

Make 6 ch and join into ring with sl st.

1st round 3 ch, 1 tr into ring, (7 ch, 2 tr in ring) 3 times, 7 ch, sl st into 3rd of 3 ch.

2nd round Sl st into next tr, sl st into next sp, 3 ch, 9 tr in same sp, (5 ch, 10 tr in next sp) 3 times, 5 ch, sl st in 3rd of 3 ch.

3rd round 3 ch, leaving last loop of each st on hook work 1 tr in each of next 4 tr, yrh and draw through all loops on hook – cluster made – *5 ch, leaving last loop of each st on hook work 1 tr in each of next 5 tr, yrh and draw through all loops on hook – 5-tr cluster made – 5 ch, in next corner loop work a 4-tr cluster, 9 ch, 4-tr cluster, 5 ch, work 5-tr cluster over next 5 tr; rep from * omitting 1 5-tr cluster at end of last rep, sl st into first cluster.

4th round *(1 dc in each of next 3 ch, 3 ch, 1 dc in same place as last dc – picot made – 1 dc in each of next 2 ch, miss next cluster) twice, 1 dc in each of next 5 ch, 3 ch, picot, 1 dc in each of next 4 ch, miss next cluster, 1 dc in each of next 3 ch, 3 ch, picot, 1 dc in each of next 2 ch, miss next cluster; rep from * ending sl st in first dc. Fasten off.

Second motif

Work first three rounds as first motif.

4th round (1 dc in each of next 3 ch, 3 ch, picot, 1 dc in each of next 2 ch, miss next cluster) twice, 1 dc in each of next 5 ch, 1 ch, sl st to corresponding picot of first motif, 1 ch, 1 dc in same place as last dc on (second motif, 1 dc in each of next 4 ch, miss next cluster, 1 dc in each of next 3 ch, 1 ch, sl st in corresponding picot of first motif, 1 ch, 1 dc in same place as last dc on second motif, 1 dc in each of next 2 ch, miss next cluster) 3 times, 1 dc in each of next 5 ch, 1 ch, sl st in corresponding picot on first motif, 1 ch, 1 dc in same place as last dc on second motif and complete as first motif.

To complete

Continue to make and join the motifs, working a row of six motifs for the width, and four rows of six motifs for the length to complete a cloth to the size shown. Each motif measures approx 7.5 cm ($2\frac{3}{4}$ in) square and the cloth measures approx 45 cm ($17\frac{1}{2}$ in) wide and 30 cm ($11\frac{3}{4}$ in) long. For a larger cloth it is preferable to work more motifs rather than alter the tension, which is particularly suitable for this type of pattern.

Press the work gently, using a damp cloth.

9 Armchair back and arm rests

66 *Crochet motifs used for armchair back and arm rests, pattern 9*

This pair of useful and attractive accessories is derived from the same motif as that of the tray cloth. These examples are shown to demonstrate that the possibilities for using the same pattern are endless. However, if you wish to try using squares for window screens, always consider whether the fabric will let sufficient light through and be prepared to experiment with the pattern, for example by trying a finer yarn or a looser tension to obtain a less dense effect.

Materials
6 balls (25 g) Twilley Lyscordet No 5 cotton
2 mm crochet hook
These quantities make one back and two arm rests.
9 balls make a sofa back and two arm rests

Measurements
Back rest, 45 cm ($17\frac{1}{2}$in) wide; 30 cm ($11\frac{3}{4}$ in) deep
Arm rest, 30 cm ($11\frac{3}{4}$ in) wide; 22.5 cm ($8\frac{1}{2}$ in) deep

To make
The single armchair back rest is made exactly as the tray cloth, crochet pattern 8. The example shown rested comfortably on the back of the chair, which was quite deep, and because of the raised nap the crochet clung well; where the back of the chair is narrow or perhaps the top is wooden or otherwise slippery, the cloth may be prevented from slipping by working twice the number of motifs and having the cloth overhanging the back and the front equally or, if preferred, two heavy tassels may be attached to the back corners to weight the back. In either case, extra yarn must be provided for this purpose.

The arm rests are made by following crochet pattern 8, but four motifs are needed for the width and three motifs for the depth (twelve motifs). On a narrow chair arm the rests will stay in place, and indeed are enhanced, if a tassel is added to each corner. (For tassel instructions see page 45).

67   Detail of crochet motif used in patterns 8 and 9

10   Bedlinen edgings

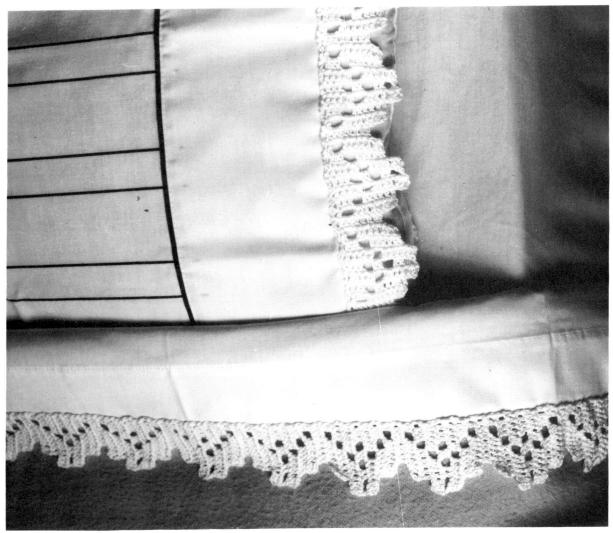

68   Crochet edging for bedlinen, pattern 10

The edging used in the photograph is neat, practical and easy to work; it has everything that is suited to a plain white or unfussy basic linen. It will wash and handle well and gives just a touch of interest to the linen.

This type of border has been chosen because it is worked widthways, forming a narrow strip in preference to working the foundation chain to the width of the sheet or pillowslip. The narrow strips can be tacked in place as you work to ensure a good fit.

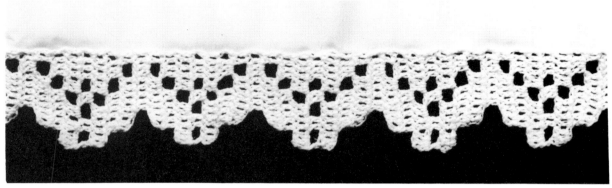

69   *Detail of crochet bedlinen edging, pattern 10*

Materials
2 balls (25 g) Twilley Lyscordet No 5 cotton to make sheet edging (see measurements)
1 ball to make one pillowslip edging
2 mm crochet hook

Measurements
5 cm (2 in) wide; sheet edging 182 cm (72 in) long; each pillowslip 102 cm (40 in) long.

Tension
A crochet hook should be used with this yarn to produce strips with a width of 5 cm (2 in).

To make
Make 11 ch.

1st row   1 tr in 4 th ch from hook, 1 tr in each ch to end, turn (*9 sts*).

2nd row   5 ch, 1 tr in 4th ch from hook, 1 tr in next ch, 1 tr in each of next 5 tr, 2 ch, miss 2 tr, 1 tr in next tr, 1 tr in top of turning ch, turn.

3rd row   3 ch (stands as first tr), miss 1 tr, 1 tr in next tr, 2 tr in 2-ch sp, 2 ch, miss 2 tr, 1 tr in each of 6 tr, turn.

4th row   5 ch, 1 tr in 4th ch from hook, 1 tr in next ch, 1 tr in each of next 4 tr, 2 ch, 2 tr in next 2-ch sp, 1 tr in each of next 3 tr, 1 tr in top of 3 ch, turn.

5th row   3 ch, miss 1st tr, 1 tr in each of next 3 tr, 2 ch, miss 2 tr, 2 tr in next 2-ch sp, 2 ch, miss 2 tr, 1 tr in each of next 2 tr, 2 ch, miss 2 tr, 1 tr in top of 3 ch, turn.

6th row   3 ch, miss 1 tr, 2 tr in 2-ch sp, 1 tr in each of next 2 tr, 2 tr in 2-ch sp, 2 ch, miss 2 tr, 2 tr in next 2-ch sp, 1 tr in each of next 3 tr, 1 tr in top of 3 ch, turn.

7th row   3 ch, miss 1 tr, 1 tr in each of next 3 tr, 2 ch, 2 tr in next 2-ch sp, 1 tr in each of next 4 tr, turn.

8th row   3 ch, miss 1 tr, 1 tr in each of next 5 tr, 2 tr in next 2-ch sp, 2 ch, miss 2 tr, 1 tr in next tr, 1 tr in top of 3 ch, turn.

9th row   3 ch, miss 1 tr, 1 tr in next tr, 2 tr in 2-ch sp, 1 tr in each of next 5 tr, turn.

The 2nd to 9th rows form the pattern. Repeat them until the strip fits, unstretched, along width of sheet or all round pillowslip opening.

To complete
Sew neatly to sheet edge or pillowslip opening. On pillowslip opening, join the first to last edges.

11   Alternative linen edgings

These edgings are as unobtrusive as the previous borders in their narrowness but offer a slightly more unusual quality.

Materials
These are similar to the linen edging requirements listed above in crochet pattern 10.

Measurements
The fan cluster pattern edging is 5 cm (2 in) wide.
The picot pattern edging is 3 cm (1¼ in) wide.
The length of the edging is optional.

70   *Crochet fan cluster linen edging, pattern 11*

To make the fan cluster edging

Make 10 ch and join into ring with sl st.

1st row   3 ch, 14 tr into ring, 5 ch, turn.

2nd row   Miss first tr, (1 tr in next tr, 2 ch, miss 1 tr) 6 times, 1 tr in top of 3 ch, turn.

3rd row   *7 tr in next sp, remove hook from loop, insert hook into top of 3 ch then into the dropped loop and draw through all loops – cluster made – 3 ch; rep from * 5 times more, 1 cluster in last sp, 10 ch, turn.

4th row   Miss first 2 sps, (1 dc, 5 ch, 1 dc) all in next sp, 3 ch, turn.

5th row   13 tr in 5-ch loop, 1 dc in 10-ch loop, 5 ch, turn.

6th row   Miss first dc and first tr, (1 tr in next tr, 2 ch, miss 1 tr) 6 times, 1 tr in top of 3 ch, 3 ch, turn.

Rep 3rd to 6th rows for the pattern until the strip is the required length.

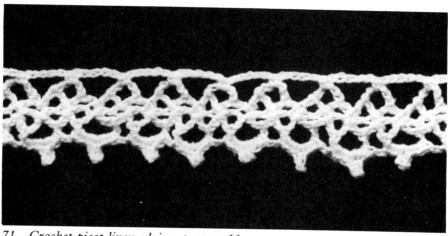

71   *Crochet picot linen edging, pattern 11*

To make the picot edging

Make 6 ch.

1st row   Into 6th ch from hook work 3 tr with 2 ch between, turn.

2nd row   Into centre tr work 3 tr with 2 ch between, 5 ch, turn.

The 2nd row forms the pattern. Rep the row until the strip is the required length. Do not turn at the end of the last row but work the heading across one long side thus:

*1 dc in next 5-ch loop, 5 ch; rep from * ending 3 ch, 1 tr in first st. Fasten off.

To make the picot edge: join the yarn to first 5-ch loop, 3 dc into loop, *4 ch, 1 dc in 4th ch from loop – picot made – 3 dc in same 5-ch loop, 2 ch, 3 dc in next 5-ch loop; rep from * ending with 3 dc, picot, 3 dc in last 5-ch loop. Fasten off.

To complete

Treat these edgings as the first border (pattern 10) and attach to the bedlinen in the same way.

12 Pram or cot cover

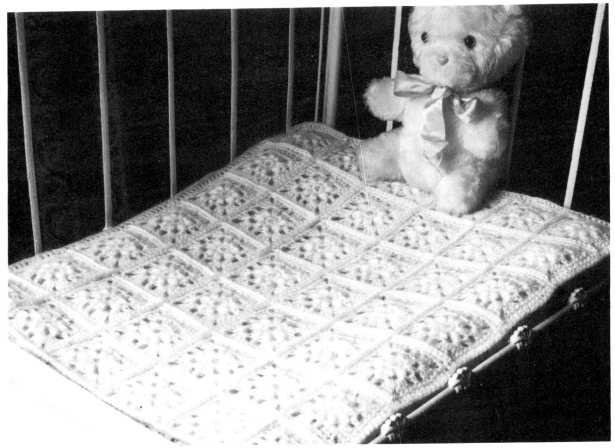

72 *Crochet pram or cot cover, pattern 12*

These small granny squares look attractive in cotton yarn for adult beds but are better suited to yarn that is soft to the touch for babies. A bonus for this type of cover is that, provided it has only lightweight wear, it is a simple matter to add more squares later to use it on the child's first grown-up size bed. Despite its delicate look the cover is worked with a thick hook and this, together with the fact that the squares are joined as you work, must make it one of the quickest gifts you could set out to make for a baby.

Materials
5 balls (50 g) Twilley Featherspun mohair-look
7 mm crochet hook

Measurements

71 cm (28 in) long; 61 cm (24 in) wide

Tension

Each square measures 10 cm (4 in) along each side edge.

To make each motif   Make 42 pieces.

Make 6 ch, join into ring with sl st.

1st round   8 dc into ring, join with sl st.

2nd round   3 ch, *leaving last loop on hook, work 2 tr in first st, yrh and draw through all loops, 3 ch, 3-tr cluster in next st, 1 ch; rep from * 3 times more, join with sl st to top of 3 ch.

3rd round   Sl st to ch sp, 3 ch (stands as 1st tr), 2 tr in same sp, 3 ch, 3 tr in same ch sp, *1 ch, miss next cluster, 1 tr in ch sp between next 2 clusters, 1 ch, 3 tr, 3 ch, 3 tr in next ch sp; rep from * 3 times, ending 1 ch, join with sl st to top of 3 ch.

4th round   With wrong sides of two motifs together, work 1 row dc along side edges to join. Fasten off.

When six squares have been joined in this way, fasten off and begin a new strip of squares.

To complete

Join the seven rows of six strips together with double crochet forming a ridge on the right side of the work as the squares are joined.

For the border, join the yarn to one corner, 3 ch, 2 tr in same corner st, work 1 tr in each st all round outer edge, working 3 tr in each corner. Fasten off. Do not press.

73   Motif for crochet pram cover, pattern 12

13   Openwork round cushion cover

74   Openwork crochet cover for round cushion, pattern 13

Although this cover is worked in bold white yarn you will be able to link it into your colour scheme by using a blending colour for the lining fabric. The circular pattern may be repeated as a tablecloth to match, by omitting the popcorn stitches and continuing the rounds until the cloth is the desired size.

Materials
3 hanks (100 g) Twilley Handicraft No 1 Cotton
4 mm crochet hook

Measurement
Diameter of cushion cover is 46 cm (18 in).

Tension
Work to the equivalent of 18 trs to 10 cm (4 in) to produce the measurements given above.

To make

Make 5 ch, join into ring with sl st.

1st round   10 dc in ring, join with sl st.

2nd round   5 ch (stands as 1 tr, 2 ch), 1 tr in next dc, 2 ch, *1 tr in next dc, 2 ch; rep from * to end, join with sl st to 3rd of 5 ch (*10 tr*).

3rd round   Sl st into first sp, 3 ch (stands as 1 tr), 3 tr in same sp, *4 tr in next sp; rep from * to end, join with sl st to top of 3 ch.

4th round   5 ch, 1 tr in first tr, *miss 1 tr, (1tr, 1 ch, 1 tr) all in next tr; rep from * to end, join with sl st to 3rd of 5 ch.

5th round   Sl st into first sp, *5 ch, miss 2 tr, 1 dc in next ch sp; rep from * to end, ending with 5 ch, join to first sp.

6th round   Sl st to first sp, 3 ch, (1 tr, 2 ch, 2 tr) in same sp, *(2 tr, 2 ch, 2 tr) in each 5-ch sp; rep from * to end, join with sl st to top of 3 ch.

7th round   Sl st into first 2-ch sp, 3 ch, (1 tr, 2 ch, 2 tr) in same sp, *(2 tr, 2 ch, 2 tr) in each 2-ch sp; rep from * to end, join with sl st to top of 3 ch.

8th round   Sl st into first 2-ch sp, into this same sp work 5 tr, remove the hook from last tr, and insert in top of first tr, then through dropped loop, yrn and draw through all loops – popcorn made – 6 ch, *1 popcorn, 6 ch; rep from * to end, join with sl st to top of first popcorn.

9th round   Sl st into first 6-ch sp, 3 ch, (2 tr, 2 ch, 3 tr) in same 6-ch sp, (3 tr, 2 ch, 3 tr) in each 6-ch sp to end, join with sl st to top of 3 ch.

10th round   7 ch, *1 dc in next 2-ch sp, 5 ch, miss 3 tr, 1 tr in sp between trs, 5 ch; rep from * to end, join with sl st to 3rd of 7 ch.

11th round   Sl st into first sp, 3 ch, *(2 tr, 2 ch, 2 tr) in next 5-ch sp, (2 tr, 2 ch, 2 tr) in next 5-ch sp, 1 tr in next tr; rep from * to end, omitting last 1 tr, join with sl st to top of 3 ch.

12 round   Sl st into first sp, 3 ch, *(2 tr, 2 ch, 2 tr) in next 2-ch sp, (2 tr, 2 ch, 2 tr) in next 2-ch sp, 1 tr in next tr; rep from * to end, omitting last 1 tr, join with sl st to top of 3 ch.

13th round   As 12th round.

14th round   *(7 ch, 1 dc in 2-ch sp) twice, 7 ch, miss 2 tr, 1 dc in next tr; rep from * ending last rep, sl st to 1st of 7 ch instead of dc in next tr.
Fasten off.

Work second piece in the same way.

To complete

Prepare cushion pad and lining. With wrong sides of crochet cover together, join yarn in a 7-ch loop, work this loop together with adjacent 7-ch loop of second side with 1 dc, *5 ch, join next two 7-ch loops with 1 dc; rep from * until approx one-third of the opening remains. Insert the cushion pad and continue joining the cover to end, ending 5 ch, join with sl st to 1st dc. Fasten off.

The cover should not need pressing but the last round may be improved by pressing to draw out these outer loops.

When removing the cushion for laundering the cover, make a note of how the two sides were joined so that they may be quickly rejoined again.

Conversion chart for knitting needles and crochet hooks

Knitting needles

UK		USA	Continental
Old sizes	Metric (mm)		(mm)
000	10	15	9
00	9	13	8·5
0	8	12	8
1	$7\frac{1}{2}$	11	7·5
2	7	$10\frac{1}{2}$	7
3	$6\frac{1}{2}$	10	6·5
4	6	9	6
5	$5\frac{1}{2}$	8	5·5
6	5	7	5
7	$4\frac{1}{2}$	6	4·5
8	4	5	4
9	$3\frac{3}{4}$	4	3·5
10	$3\frac{1}{4}$	3	–
11	3	2	3
12	$2\frac{3}{4}$	1	2·5
13	$2\frac{1}{4}$	0	–
14	2	00	2

Crochet hooks

UK (mm)	USA	Continental (mm)
7	K/$10\frac{1}{2}$	7
6·5	J/10	6·5
6	I/9	6
5·5	H/8	5·5
5	–	5
4·5	G/6	4·5
4	F/5	4
3·5	E/4	3·5
3	C/2	3
2·5	B/1	2·5
2	–	2

Glossary

Garter stitch: knit every row.

Knitwise: a term generally used in slipping stitches from the left-hand needle to the right by inserting the point of the right-hand needle into the loop, as if to knit it.

Purlwise: slipping a stitch from the left-hand needle to the right by inserting the point of the right-hand needle into the loop, as if to purl it.

Pass the slipped stitch over: the slipped stitch(es) is the first to be passed on to the right-hand needle; insert the point of the left-hand needle into this loop and lift it over the last stitch(es) on right-hand needle and off the needle.

Seed stitch: moss stitch, the method worked by reversing the k1 and p1 on consecutive rows.

Stocking stitch: stockinette, worked by one row knit, followed by one row purl.

Tension, gauge: the number of stitches and/or rows measured to a given number of centimetres or inches.

Through back of loop: knit or purl through the back of the stitch instead of the front; to knit, this means inserting the point of the right-hand needle into the centre of the loop from the right-hand side through to the back; to purl, this means inserting the point of the right-hand needle from the back from the left-hand side. The same technique is used for working two stitches together through back of loops.

*: this asterisk indicates the beginning of a pattern repeat; a semi-colon indicates the conclusion.

( ): brackets (parentheses) are used within pattern repeats where the method contained within the brackets is to be worked for the number of times indicated immediately following the bracket signs, e.g. (k2 tog) twice.

Yarn forward: a method of making a stitch by bringing the yarn forward between two knit stitches and over the top of the needle to work the following knit stitch.

Yarn round needle: this is the method of making a stitch when the yarn is already in the forward position and a purl stitch follows.

Crochet terms

UK	USA
double crochet	single crochet
half treble	half double crochet
treble	double crochet
double treble	treble
triple treble	double treble

Bibliography

Abbey, Barbara, *Knitting Lace*, The Viking Press Inc., New York, 1974
Stearns, Ann, *The Batsford Book of Crochet*, Batsford, 1981
Thomas, Mary, *Book of Knitting Patterns*, Hodder and Stoughton, 1935

Suppliers

To obtain information about stockists in the United Kingdom write to the following addresses:

For Twilley yarns (used throughout the book)
H. G. Twilley Ltd
Roman Mill
Stamford
Lincs
PE9 1BG

J. & P. Coats Ltd also specialise in cotton yarns but it is difficult to recommend exact alternatives. Readers are advised to work a tension sample before starting on any item.

J. & P. Coats Ltd
Domestic Marketing Division
Market Service Dept
39 Durham Street
Glasgow
G41 1BS

For Bond Knitting Systems
Bond Knitting Systems Ltd
79 High Street
Witney
Oxon
OX8 6LR

Index

Pages where illustrations appear are listed in *italic*.